D0822997

Borderline Brainwashed

by Sarah the Human

to my parents who taught me their truth

to my siblings who are my light

Contents

Rebranding

This may come as a shock, but Sarah the Human is not my legal name. It's Sarah Blake. The name Sarah Blake was taken by Sarah Blake, author of The Guest House, and it is still a sensitive subject. With my legal name off the table, I was forced to brainstorm pseudonyms. Oddly enough, the idea of inventing an alias sounded attractive. I was peeved all right that Sarah Blake was in use, don't get me wrong, but the unlimited possibilities of what my new name could be intrigued me.

This is not the first time I have rebranded. Prior to marrying the love of my life, Beau Blake, my name was Sarah Girouard. Girouard was ruled out as a suitable pen name as it is confusing as all get out to spell for anyone who is not French. There are three vowels in a row, for heaven's sake! Besides, I had been a Girouard for many, many years. Twenty-two, to be exact. Putting on that name again would feel like a step backward because I'd been there, done that. I wanted something unworn. Something crisp.

Transitioning from Girouard to Blake was clunky. For starters, you have the legal hassle. I took two trips to hell and back (aka the Department of Motor Vehicles) to renew my driver's license and switch my social security card. Somehow, some five years later, the name next to my passport photo is still Sarah Girouard. Apologies to the TSA.

Then you have social confusion. On the regular I signed receipts at checkouts with the wrong last name. Do you ever in the new year accidentally write the date as the old year? Like that. For months I experienced mad imposter syndrome responding to Mrs. Blake. Mrs. Blake? Who the fudge is that? It was awkward modifying my identity because at first I didn't feel like my new name suited me. According to the government, I was a Blake, yes, yet I couldn't help but still feel like a Girouard. Girouard was comfortable, similar to a favorite pair of sneakers. I got spick-and-span, fresh kicks, but part of me missed my raggedy Converse.

Apparently, I wasn't the only person struggling to adapt. My dad, who used to call me Sarah G., had trouble breaking the habit. He'd realize his mistake, apologize, and correct himself to Sarah B. (In Dad's defense, Gee and Bee are easy to mix up.) Some of my friends said they would refer to me as Sarah Girouard by accident when I came up in conversation. And there were people in my life who did not bother, refused even, to update my contact info in their cell phones.

What I find to be even more bizarre, by far, is when I've met and befriended folks post-marriage. These people had never even heard of Sarah Girouard. It's like the old me, who I was for 22 years, never existed. Do I tell them about my other name? Do I reveal or conceal my past identity? Both options feel weird. It's at these points that I was tempted to forget the whole name change. Can't I just regress to how things were before?

If you've ever made a practically permanent change, you know how daunting it is to retrace your steps. Returning a car, for instance, is much more of a feat after you've signed the title than if you never purchased it originally. Moving back to your hometown is also much more of an ordeal than if you never left to begin with. Reverting a legal name to the name on your birth certificate is much more strenuous than if you never edited it in the first place. I, for one, was not about to endure the lines at the DMV all over again. Once you've made a practically permanent change, it feels nearly impossible to jump ship. And it's unnerving.

The name Blake scared me because it was an experimental territory. On day one of Blake, I was someone I had never been as Girouard: a wife. On day 14 of Blake, I moved somewhere I had visited once as Girouard: Los Angeles. The name Girouard had all of my belongings attached to it. Baggage, but belongings nonetheless. At least I knew who I was supposed to be as Girouard: outgoing, fun, cute, courteous, Conservative, Fundamentalist Christian. What made Sarah Blake Sarah Blake was yet to be determined.

Despite the crippling self-consciousness, I chose to use a new identity outwardly as an opportunity to reinvent myself inwardly. I stepped into the discomfort and opened up my heart for a renovation. I let habits, thoughts, ideas, fears and beliefs that were no longer serving me fizzle out. As a result, everything shifted. And I mean everything. My religion, politics, interests, fashion, taste in music, mind, body and heart. Everything. In time, I transformed into a completely different person, a person Sarah Girouard would not recognize.

After a while, I got used to being a Blake. I got so used to it that the name Blake began to feel more like me than Girouard ever did. The process, angsty as it was, paid off. Eventually, I became Sarah Blake. My loved ones adjusted too, mostly. Slowly friends and family started to view me as the new name and not the old name. Literally and metaphorically. Just in time for me to take on another new name: Sarah the Human.

I'm in the midst of breaking in Sarah the Human. Thankfully, I won't get the government involved with this name switch. I will, however, update my Instagram handle, which is arguably just as life-altering. Plus, think of all the paperbacks that will be printed with this pseudonym on their spines. All of those books are forever marked with my new, new identity.

To me, Sarah the Human sounds like a step into the unknown. Exhilarating, but I have no idea what's about to happen. I'm on the edge of my seat. Sarah the Human feels like me—but me in the future. Yet to be determined. On day one of Sarah the Human I am in a profession Blake had only dreamed of: author. It'll take some getting used to. And like last time, I am using this transformation on the outside to transform on the inside.

You'd think after going through reinvention once, it'd get easier the second time. Negative. I find myself again feeling weird in the "just after" phase of a practically permanent change. This go-round, Blake is what's more comfortable. Blake is what is safe. There's always a pull to go back to what is safe. Nevertheless, l am prepared to make like the sand and shift with the waves. Because on top of the weirdness, there is another through-line in rebranding (and this one is sparkly): I know another transition will lead me to a truer version of myself. Sarah Girouard was me,

Sarah Blake was more me, and Sarah the Human will be even more me. All the newness is permitting a more true me to make an appearance. The "just after" period of a practically permanent change can be both unsettling and worthwhile.

Perhaps you can't relate to having three names. But perhaps you relate to feeling out of sorts during a transitional phase, a time in which you, too, were in the weeds. In the thick of it. Or, perhaps you relate to feeling more like yourself than you have in years past. My guess is that to get to where you are now, you had to let habits, thoughts, ideas, fears, and beliefs taper off. I bet you had to thank the past versions of yourself, say your goodbyes and move on. You had to face the hard stuff in order to grow. You wouldn't be you without the tough shit. You wouldn't be you without the grit.

In this book we're going to take a hard look at our beliefs, even the ones we are unaware of. I'm not going to lie to you, things could get tough; pushing past the comfort of staying the same is risky, and where there's risk, there's grit. But where there's grit, there's growth.

I believe our world is lacking in safe spaces, so I hope to have created one. This is a judgment-free zone where no question is off-limits. Please, come inside. Pull up a chair, make yourself at home. Dishes are in the sink. My bed is not made. My plants are days away from dying. It's a little messy, but you are getting the real me. And you can be the real you. Together, we will peel back the layers of our upbringings and current environments. No matter how thick those layers are, you will discover the humanness at your core. A more true you will emerge.

As you read, I encourage you to think for yourself. Block out what your pastor preaches or what your grandfather teaches. Try not to think about what your best friend would say or how your significant other would react. What do *you* think about all of this? You see, when you evolve, not all of your loved ones are going to get it. There will be people in your world who refuse to update your new name in their phone contacts, if you know what I mean. Folks are going to treat you like you're the old you when you're the new you. It's an adjustment for all. It's an adjustment to which most are bound to adapt after enough time has passed. Just in time for you to become the next you.

The question is not *if* evolution awaits you on the other side of deconstructing your beliefs. The question is: are you ready for the transformation? Because chances are, you, like me, have been borderline brainwashed.

In the Beginning

For eight out of 12 grades I was homeschooled. In my hometown of Little Rock, Arkansas, homeschooling is quite common. Arkansas's public school system is just shy of being the worst in America, ranking 42 out of the 50 states (50 being the worst). If your parents did not have the wallets for private school, homeschooling was the next best option.

The thing about homeschooling is that you can march to the beat of your own drum. You (the parent) are in charge of your own schooling schedule, including which holidays you observe. As long as your kid scores okay on the mandated standardized tests, you can pretty much teach whatever you want. It's all very flexible. A casual teaching style worked well for my creative mom. She got to add her own personal flair to the curriculum.

My mom, a Fundamentalist Christian, disagreed with what science textbooks taught regarding the origins of our planet. As a replacement lesson, I was instructed to write a book report on the first few chapters of Genesis. The Bible educated elementary school me on Earth's first humans, Adam and Eve, and how God said "Let there be light," and there was light.

Oftentimes the Old and New Testaments sufficed for history lessons, too. While most fifth-graders memorized American Presidents, I memorized the Book of Job. While most middle schoolers learned about Abraham Lincoln, I learned about John the Baptist. Not sure if you know this, but the Bible does not touch on World War I, World War II or Valley Forge. To this day, I am missing chunks of history knowledge. At least I can name the 12 tribes of Judah.

Growing up in a church community, the teachings of the Bible were reiterated constantly. In Sunday School, I colored pictures of the Garden of Eden. I watched *Jonah: A VeggieTales Movie* at friends' houses, and listened to Christian artists like DC Talk and Newsboys.

On Wednesdays, I attended AWANA, a Scripture memorization program for young tykes. AWANA stands for Approved Workmen [Who] Are Not Ashamed (of the gospel of Christ). I made for a proud seven-year-old, dressed in my royal blue vest, acquiring its iron-on patches that were rewarded for reciting verses I'd successfully committed to memory. The meetings kicked off with an assembly of us vested kiddos standing side by side, hands on our hearts. We pledged our allegiances to the American Flag—because Jesus was a patriot—and the AWANA Flag.

> I pledge allegiance to the Awana flag, which
>
> stands for the Awana Clubs, whose goal is to
>
> reach boys and girls with the gospel of Christ,
>
> and train them to serve Him.

You see, Fundamentalist Christianity was less of an option and more of an indoctrination. When your parents, pastors, AWANA leaders, and friends proclaim the same message, you adopt it, no questions asked. I was conditioned by my authority figures and peers to accept Fundamentalist Christian views as capital T *Truth* and categorize individuals who don't as *lost*. It was an "it is what it is" mentality. Simply exploring other theories of the Earth's formation felt like free soloing El Capitan. Reckless. The opposite of grounded. If I were to entertain the possibility of The Big Bang, it'd be a betrayal. A scandal. Questioning was out of the question.

Surprisingly enough, this blind-follower energy worked great until I hit my mid-20s and started to have—wait for it—questions. The problem that comes with being borderline brainwashed is you feel guilty for questioning. Which, if you think about it, makes total sense. The people who told you the stuff you now have doubts about are likely your family members. I mean, they are the people who provided you with food and shelter, bathed you and changed your freaking diapers. How are you supposed to rock the boat when your dad, your caregiver, is steering the boat?

It's likely that if our loved ones believe something, we'll end up believing it, too. Thus, it can feel impossible to go against the grain. All of us were born into *something*. Christian, Jewish, Muslim, Mormon, Hindu, Conservative, Liberal, hippie—you get the picture. All of us were born into something, even if that something is nothing. Sorry Atheists, a belief system founded on no God can be as influential as a belief system founded on a higher power. Whatever the case, how we were brought up shaped us big time.

Experts say that the majority of our beliefs as adults stem from our environment growing up. It's as if our beliefs from early years stuck to us like sticky glue. I don't know about you, but I can still hear my mom saying, "Nothing good happens after midnight," or instructing me to take my elbows off the table. And I'm going on five years married, an adult with a child (cat) of my own. Our parents taught us to believe the same things they did about what makes a man a man or a woman a woman. How we should vote was ingrained in our very being. Even our likes and dislikes, from sports to dance to music to what foods we prefer, have been influenced by how and where we were raised.

Israeli psychologist and 2002 Nobel Laureate Daniel Kahneman said, "For some of our most important beliefs, we have no evidence at all, except that people we love and trust hold these beliefs. Considering how little we know, the confidence we have in our beliefs is preposterous."[i]

Yikes.

Studies say that we develop core beliefs during childhood. Core beliefs are a person's most principal ideas about themselves, others and the world. The crux of our belief framework accumulates from the models around us—moms, dads, grandpas, grandmas, teachers, so on and so forth—and accompanies us well into adulthood.

Core beliefs re: yourself

- I am accepted.

- I am a failure.

- I am inherently good.

- I am inherently bad.

Core beliefs re: others

- You can trust people.

- You cannot trust people.

- People are inherently good.

- People are inherently bad.

Core beliefs re: the world

- The world is a safe place.

- The world is a dangerous place.

- The world is getting better with time.

- The world is getting worse with time.

Core beliefs are so central to who we are that putting them into question would considerably rearrange how we see life. Therefore, it is probable that we never put them into question. To reiterate: it's likely we *never* question the core beliefs we were handed in childhood. Is it just me or is that wild?

Psychotherapist Amy Morin said, "Letting go of unproductive core beliefs you developed during childhood can be the key to moving forward and reaching your greatest potential."[ii] Beliefs are the lens through which we interpret our reality. If that lens is blurred, we may be interpreting our reality in a wonky manner. It's important to put beliefs in check because beliefs are the driving factors behind our actions and behaviors— and oftentimes, beliefs turn into self-fulfilling prophecies.

Core beliefs re: influencing actions

- If I believe a potential partner will be unfaithful, I will not download dating apps.

- If I believe I am dumb, I will not put much effort into academia.

- If I believe I am accepted, I will enter a room with confidence.

Core beliefs re: self-fulling prophecies

- If I do not download dating apps, I am less likely to meet a loyal partner.

- If I do not put much effort into academia, I become dumb when I wasn't before.

- If I enter a room with confidence, I am likely to be accepted by my peers.

Via homeschooling, AWANA, church retreats, youth groups, mission trips and more, I formed a good chunk of my beliefs from the literal interpretation of the Bible. And by a good chunk, I mean around 88 percent, if I had to put a percentage on it. On top of science and history courses, I consulted Scripture for explanations on anything and everything. It was my answer sheet for what to make of myself, others and the world.

Well into adulthood, I discovered I held multiple unhealthy core beliefs which led to unconstructive behaviors and negative self-fulfilling prophecies. The lens I was looking through was fogged. I couldn't see straight, so I bumped into things and people, collecting metaphorical bruises wherever I went. For a long period of time, I had no clue I was damaging my body, mind and spirit. That is until I put my core beliefs into question.

If you were born into Scientology or joined a cult, like NXIVM, you were legitimately brainwashed. If that is the case, my heart goes out to you. Truly. As for everyone else, you, like me, were not brainwashed *per se*. Not quite, but along those lines. Borderline brainwashed. Either way, it could be that you are 100 percent on board with your upbringing. But my guess is there is a percentage of you that cannot get behind *everything*. There are elements about it that do not sit right. Some things do not add up. Deep down, you have some questions.

When you have questions, avoidance and suppression only work for so long. Eventually, the questions you have will multiply and bubble over. I will confess, it's *risky* and treacherous to ask complicated or controversial questions. Yet if we avoid friction, we become blind followers, and if we're not careful, we could lose ourselves in a pack mentality. So, what is the real hazard here? Confrontation or losing yourself?

Here's the part that might make you a little squeamish. (I warned you, this stuff is uncomfy.) Unlearning and deconstructing what you believe could cost you. The way you currently view yourself, others and the world could completely shatter. How's that for some encouragement? The thing is, though, if you don't unlearn, it could cost you even more: your true self.

Avocados

I'd never tasted avocado until I was 23 years old. Avocados were not all the rage in Little Rock, Arkansas, particularly not in the late '90s and early 2000s. My mom's idea of cooking was microwaving bacon and cracking open a can of Pillsbury Flaky Layers. Dad was frugal. Generous, but frugal. On the rare occasion he took our family of six out to a restaurant, it was either CiCi's Pizza, Chili's, or, for special occasions, Macaroni Grill.

All of this to say, I seldom came into contact with avocados while living in Little Rock. If I did, it was in the form of guacamole, and without giving guac a chance, I assumed with deep-rooted conviction that it wasn't for me. *The texture.*

In 2016, my best-friend-slash-husband, Beau and I uprooted ourselves from the Bible Belt and moved to another world: Los Angeles. Avocados are everywhere in SoCal. After moving, I found it increasingly difficult to avoid them. In settings like hip coffee shops and restaurants, avos are an ingredient in almost every item on the menus. Saying, "No avocado, please," each time I placed an order for sushi, salad or a burger got real old real fast.

Gradually over the first six months residing in LA, my firmly-established anti-avo belief loosened up. Sick of feeling like a picky eater and often hearing, "What do you mean you don't like avocados?", California culture influenced me to give them a shot. I caved, eventually, and decided it was time to get a taste of the unknown.

I started small by scooping out teeny chunks into my morning smoothies. Then I graduated to making homemade guac with extra tomatoes and extra onions to lessen the sliminess. The straight-up slices freaked me out the most, so I doused them in olive oil and added spices like sea salt and chili flakes. Slowly, I made my way through three tiers: avos as a mix-in, then a dip, and lastly, as is. In a matter of weeks, I went from having a phobia to having an addiction.

In the fall of 2020, arguably the worst year of human existence, I had an itch to take a solo vacation. The external world and my internal world were in a state of total chaos. I had a lot to process and wanted to rid myself of distractions. I needed no friends, no plans, no nothing. Masked up, I flew from one Covid hotspot (Los Angeles) to another: New York City. I checked into the Arlo Hotel in SoHo and did not come out for five days. More or less.

The Arlo was a vibe. Its rooftop restaurant is where I spent most of my time reading and writing and eating and drinking. One evening on the roof, the temp was sixty degrees and breezy—which felt like below zero for this Angeleno. I sipped a $19 margarita and single-handedly took down an order of tortilla chips and—you guessed it—guac. Cross-legged and bundled up, I giggled to myself about how guacamole is legitimately my favorite food. Thinking about how I used to believe I didn't like avocados made me smirk. That's when I had this thought: what else do I believe that I think is true and is not?

Stanford psychology professor Carol Dweck found that people have one of two mindsets: a fixed mindset or a growth mindset. A person with a fixed mindset wants to appear as if they have it all figured out. It is nearly impossible for a fixed-mindset person to entertain new beliefs or make edits to old ones. A fixed-mindset person avoids any and all scenarios or environments that will put what they think they know to be true to the test.

Dweck thinks that if we want to grow, we need to develop a growth mindset. A person with a growth mindset welcomes opportunities that will challenge their existing beliefs, and views the world as an endless learning tool. They hold their thoughts and opinions with an open hand. Even if it shatters their current worldview, growth-mindset people open themselves up to receiving novel ideas. Dweck said, "Mindsets are just beliefs. They're powerful beliefs, but they're just something in your mind, and you can change your mind."[iii]

I will say, getting over a fixed mindset is no joke. It's one of those processes that are easier said than done. First, we must intentionally insert ourselves into settings that will challenge us. A change in environment was all it took for me to organically be peer pressured into giving avocados a try. Second, we must be willing to disagree with ourselves, which sucks. Admitting we were wrong is humbling. As soon as I started incorporating avos into my diet, I felt ashamed. For most of my life, I'd paraded around saying I didn't like them... and now I did?

The first few times I ordered guacamole, Beau said in an I-told-you-so voice, "I thought you didn't like avocados." Me: *sticks tongue out*

Talk about embarrassing. And that's just avocados. Can you imagine how mortifying it would be to unfix your mindset about being a Republican or a Democrat? Can you imagine how humiliating it would be to unfix your mindset about being a Baptist or a Catholic?

Oftentimes we go so far as to *identify* with our beliefs, core or miniature. Identifying with what we believe sounds nice in theory, but the issue is if we ever want to reshape a belief, it's going to feel like a betrayal to our very being. The longer we associate our person with our beliefs, the harder it will be to let go of them. In most cases, we tie ourselves to beliefs we are confident we will believe for the rest of our lives. But what if you believe something that you think is true—and it's not?

Psychiatrist Ralph Lewis said,

[An] important factor accounting for resistance to changing our beliefs is the way our beliefs are so often intertwined with how we define ourselves as people… we want to feel that we are consistent, with our behavior aligning with our beliefs. We constantly try to rationalize our own actions and beliefs and try to preserve a consistent self-image. It's embarrassing and quite often costly in a variety of ways to admit that we are fundamentally wrong.[iv]

A growth mindset welcomes a dynamic future. Sacrificing our pride is a small price to pay to trade fine for great, good to zestful, agreeable to splendiferous. Just opening myself up to something as teeny weeny as avocados brought about a much more enjoyable life with an estimated one million more dishes to try.

The only thing that had prevented me from experiencing daily yumminess was me. What other aspects of this beautiful life have I yet to tap into due to a fixed mindset?

A growth mindset is vital in the context of what we believe. Making moves towards a growth mindset means coming to terms with both disagreeing with yourself and potentially being made fun of by people who knew you pre-avocado. If you can move past yourself, the others will follow suit. Give them some time and they'll get over it. They'll get used to the new you. Usually. *winky face*

I want to stress that in most cases, cracking fixed mindsets does not happen overnight. Avocados were not love-at-first-taste; it took me more than a few nibbles to get over the mental hurdles I'd built. A change of mindset or belief is often similar in process to water dripping onto a rock. At first, the splashes of water do not make a difference. But over time, the water can change the shape of the rock. Trying new things repeatedly is a sure-fire way to uncover likes and dislikes we didn't know even we had.

If you are like me and can look back on past versions of yourself and giggle, it means you are growing. It means you are steps closer to evolving into your true self. Let me be the first to congratulate you. Kudos. Mad props. Do you know what's cool?

One day you are going to look back on who you are now and chuckle. The future you will look back at the present you and grin in kindness.

Now, does the very thought of that occurring make you want to hide? Same. The thought of my future self blushing at my present self makes me want to remain unchanged to prevent me from future self-consciousness. Like if I don't change anything too bold or shocking, I can't call myself out in years to come. But you know what? Disagreeing with ourselves is worth it to put on a growth mindset because a growth mindset leads to a truer version of ourselves. I think I'll take the embarrassment if it means getting to a more *me* me.

Sticky Note

I got a sticky note for my Sweet 16. It didn't matter to me that most of my high school friends received a car or cash on their 16th birthdays. I adored my gift; it was exactly what I'd begged my parents for. The morning of the big day, I awoke to Mom whipping up a tasty birthday breakfast—microwaved bacon and Pillsbury biscuits, of course. I took a seat at the bar and my parents, all grins, handed me the sticky note. It read: "Now that you are 16, we will allow you to read *Harry Potter*." I was ecstatic.

To be clear, my parents did not give me the Harry Potter books. No, the present was their blessing. It was one thing to permit their eldest daughter (moi) to explore the demonic world of witchcraft and wizardry, but it would be another thing to enable. Baby steps.

Now, before receiving this priceless present from the parentals, I had plenty of opportunities to rebel. I was tempted to read HP in secret after my parents went to sleep. It would have been easy, either I'd check out the books from the library or borrow them from my best friend Jenna who owned the first three. (Clearly, I gave this a lot of thought.) I just knew I would not be able to enjoy the HP experience if I had to disobey my mom and dad in order to do what I wanted. Harry Potter would be tainted with the stomach-churning feeling of knowing I was letting Mom and Dad down.

In a way, that sticky note gave me more independence than a sedan would have. It represented the freedom for me to savor one of life's little joys without the unnerving possibility of getting punished for doing so. It meant the world that my parents no longer viewed my infatuation with HP as evil (not an exaggeration!); Mom and Dad decided to accept me for me, wizardly interests and all.

I could fill an encyclopedia with a list of forbidden entertainment in the Girouard household. *Hercules, That's So Raven, Shrek, Rugrats, SpongeBob, Spirit,* etc., all banned in the name of God. Apparently, too, God did not want me to trade Pokémon cards or listen to Britney Spears.

This might sound a bit odd to you (it sounds a bit odd to me too now), but I didn't think much of it then because in Arkansas, hella conservative parenting was the norm. One of my BFFs from childhood, Megan, wasn't allowed to say the word "awesome" unless used in reference to God. Callie, another friend, had to pass a modesty check before leaving her house. (A modesty check is when you bend over and touch your toes to make sure the shirt you're wearing doesn't reveal too much of your lower back.)

As much as I hate to admit it, part of me enjoyed a regimented universe. I may have been deprived of R-rated comedies and *NSYNC, but I had no shortage of structure. The guidelines gave me a sense of control. I knew exactly what I needed to do and not do in order to please both my parents and God.

By the time I moved out from under my parents' roof, I had the "dos" ingrained in my brain: pray, read the Bible, get baptized, go to church, vote Republican, listen to Lecrae, and share the gospel with non-Christians. The "don'ts" included but were not limited to: don't have sex before marriage, don't be gay, don't smoke pot, don't get drunk, don't get tattoos, don't use curse words and don't get your cartilage pierced.

Most of my friends rebelled against conservatism when they got to college. I leaned into it. Hardcore. Fundamentalism became less of a religion and more of an identity. The dos and don'ts were familiar, a safe haven. I couldn't picture life without directions, so I strived to follow, dead on, the set I was given. Besides, it takes more resolve, wherewithal and guts to break the rules than it does to keep them. Strength was not my strong suit; fragility was my expertise.

With full conviction, I believed each directive in the Bible, especially the ones recorded in the New Testament, to be directives from God. To me, the words in the Bible, though written by humans, equaled God's words. Therefore, if God made the rules, wouldn't He be a little disappointed if I broke one? Or wouldn't He be a little proud if I didn't? If I told someone about Jesus, I imagined God saying, "Well done my good and faithful servant." If I led a Bible study, He'd add a jewel to my crown in heaven. But if I forgot to pray, it'd upset Him. If I said the F-word, He'd dock me three points.

Pleasing God was a driving factor behind my behaviors. In fact, I viewed pleasing God as the entire purpose of my existence, and I was after an A-plus. God wanted me to tithe, so I tithed. God didn't want me to party in school, so I didn't party in school. Depending on how I behaved, I felt like God either loved me more or less. My self-worth was tied to how I imagined God viewed me and that generated a constant strive for perfection.

In the spring of 2020, my hair started falling out. I'm not one of those gals whose Ariel hair routinely clogs the drain, so this was highly abnormal. Ultra-thin as my hair is, I cannot afford to lose any strands. To make matters worse, at the same time, my face turned into a canvas of red polka-dots. I'd experienced a little pimple here and there, but not anything this puss-filled and perpetual. Both my hair and skin freaked out.

I tried all the home remedies. I practiced yoga and meditation to help with stress (after all, it was 2020). I eliminated certain foods from my diet. I tried washing my hair. I tried not washing my hair. I tried washing my face. I tried not washing my face. All to no avail. My symptoms intensified.

Defeated, I sought advice from my wellness guru and friend, Katie. The two of us grabbed coffees to-go and took a socially distanced stroll through West Hollywood. Oat cappuccino in hand, Katie asked me when I'd last gotten my period. My period? What does my period have to do with my hair and skin?

Turns out, Katie was on to something: 14 months prior, I'd stopped taking birth control. I expected my natural cycle to kick back in after a few months, but it didn't. Katie, having been through a similar journey, suspected the hair loss and acne stemmed from a hormonal imbalance. Upon hearing her suggestions for how to resolve my troubles, my heart sank. In order to get my natural flow back, I would have to face my worst fear: gaining weight.

Though nearly oblivious to it, for almost a decade I had suffered from an eating disorder. From the outside, I didn't appear anorexic, but on the inside, I was sickly. I was sneaky about it. So sneaky, in fact, I fooled myself into thinking my relationship with food was unproblematic. I either ate too little or nothing at all. And just when I felt like I was going to pass out, I would surrender and overeat.

It was a constant battle for control. I legit thought starving myself was healthy. Every other week, I persevered through multi-day juice cleanses or detoxed with lemon water. I was either cleansing or intermittent fasting or on a restrictive diet like Paleo or Whole30. Then, like clockwork, I'd binge eat. You can only survive off kale for so long. Gimme all the chocolate and Flaming Hot Cheetos.

My body was over it and mad at me for being malnourished. It didn't have the energy to produce a period because it was too busy trying to keep me alive. My hormones decided to cause a scene, hence the thinning hair and acne. Katie recommended I eat 2500-3000 calories a day (no workouts!) for three months straight. She said if I wanted my body to generate a period, I'd need to gain at least 10-15 pounds. *Sooo*, actualize my biggest nightmare? Cool, cool.

Despite a number of hesitations, I decided to give it a go. After 60 days of stuffing my tummy and sitting on my butt, my body healed itself. Like magic, my cycle regulated, my hair thickened and my face cleared. I identified and tackled the root cause of my issues, and the symptoms dissolved. Focusing my attention on solving my physical problems brought my mental and emotional ones into the light. Recognizing I had a problem caused me to look within. *Why was I treating myself so poorly?*

Do you remember how our core beliefs affect the way we see ourselves? Immersed in a world of religious strictness, I developed two harmful core beliefs about myself: I am not accepted as I am, and I am inherently bad (a sinner). Viewing myself in a negative light was the root cause of my sickness. Studies say it's quite common for adults who come from rigid backgrounds to struggle with perfectionism. Perfectionism is sly because it sounds kind of cute, but in actuality it can be a terribly harmful habit. It's basically insecurity in disguise. Living a life of perfectionism and insecurity is not freeing. Some traits of perfectionism are low self-esteem, all-or-nothing thinking, unrealistic expectations, fear of failure, people-pleasing, defensiveness and being highly critical of themselves and others. Any of those characteristics ring a bell? All of the above for me.

For eight years, I believed my worthiness was tied to being stick thin with a six-pack. I only felt good about myself on the days I "performed well" and ate one stalk of celery. My confidence was shot as soon as I ate a Pringle. I legitimately thought I'd be unworthy of love if I gained 10-15 pounds. I was my worst critic by far and often compared my body to the world's most unrealistic beauty standards. Cyclically, I forced my body into submission and did not permit myself to intake what my body hungered for. Thinking I was unaccepted resulted in me having a literal distorted perspective of myself—body dysmorphia.

Another symptom of this illness reared its ugly head in my relationship with God. In his letter to the Ephesians, Paul calls on Christians to "Be imitators of Christ." Because I believed Paul's words equaled God's words, and I believed Christ to be flawless, I was convinced God wanted me to strive for flawlessness. The problem was my definition of perfection was unattainable. My idea of a perfect person was someone who never complains, worries, gossips, curses, gets frustrated, and so on. If I let out a little road rage, boom, I was heinous, ghastly and horrible.

Worse, I thought being perfect meant I had to always put my own needs last. Rather than resting to fill up my tank, I ran on empty, serving others under the illusion that I was making God happy. Slowly burying myself for the sake of being "good" led to a cycle of lashing out in moments when the torment of being a prim princess was not sustainable.

I felt I had to be obedient, spineless, a prudish person living a life I didn't choose in exchange for the approval of the Big Guy Upstairs. I wasn't free to do what I wanted without the stomach-churning feeling that God would be disappointed in me, and without the unnerving possibility of getting spiritually reprimanded for doing so. I had developed a severe lack of self-confidence and did not trust myself. My fear was this: if I took responsibility for my decisions, opinions, actions, words and *beliefs*, wouldn't that be *bad*?

In the same vein, I was afraid if I allowed my body to eat whatever it wanted, my diet would consist entirely of pancakes and Wendy's chicken nuggets. Ironically, I discovered the opposite to be true; as soon as I permitted my body to have cake whenever, wherever, with zero restrictions, I found that I only wanted cake a healthy, rare amount. Listening to my body showed me that my body knows what's up all on its own. It doesn't need me to be the gatekeeper of which foods can pass through. I allowed my body to be a body and found that it was good.

I decided to see what would happen if I let go of desperately trying to be like Jesus. I stopped miserably trying to perform and instead, authorized myself to roam free. Meaning, say no to hangs I do not have the bandwidth for, stop going to church on the

Sundays I don't want to, cuss when I stub my toe, order *two* margaritas, and watch every episode of *Euphoria* because who cares how many sex scenes are in it?

In letting loose, I found that natural consequences are baked into the universe already. I *want* to stop myself from drinking too much because if I don't, I'll wake up with a gnarly hangover the next day. I *want* to pay for the car behind me in the drive-thru because it brings me joy. I *want* to be a kind person of my own prerogative because I suffer the most from being a total jerk. As soon as I ripped the carpet of rules and regulations out from beneath me, I discovered how much more capacity I had to love others *well* because, finally, I was loving *myself* well. I gave myself the freedom to be me and the me that I found was good.

In no longer being driven to earn approval from an outside source, I found approval from within. I deconstructed my long-held core beliefs that I was not accepted and that I was a sinner. I flipped those narratives upside down. Choosing to love me as I am felt like God gave me a sticky note that read, "You are free to eat, say, think, ask, *do* whatever you want. You are accepted and always have been. You are loved and always have been. You are wanted, you are known, you are beautiful. You are worthy. You don't have to prove anything. You don't have to perform in a certain way. You can relax, take the pressure off. Exhale. Enjoy life. Just be you. Be true to yourself. You are good."

People are not one thing. There's a lot going on in our hearts. There's warmth, gentleness, patience, yuckiness, darkness, light, love, power, peace. We're the yin and yang. Humanity is a paradox. We are living, breathing contradictions cohabiting in the world. Joy and grief can coexist, as can anger and empathy. Think about the purest, newly born humans. Isn't it magical how we don't have to teach an infant to cry *and* we don't have to teach an infant to laugh? Babies express themselves by releasing their feelings of irritation *and* sheer happiness automatically. Do you view babies as bad? Or do you view babies as good? Tears and all?

It matters what we choose to believe about ourselves because, as I mentioned before, our beliefs influence our behaviors and have the potential to be self-fulfilling. If you believe you are trash, you are prone to treat yourself like trash. And when you treat yourself like trash, you are probably going to end up being a meanie head to others. But when you operate from a place of believing you are worthy of love, you are prone to taking care of yourself. And when you take care of yourself, your capacity for self-love and loving others expands.

Depending on how you view yourself, you could unknowingly be holding yourself back from a limitless life. When we view ourselves as bad, insecurities and negative thought patterns bog us down and lead us to behave in an unhealthy manner. Plus, that type of thinking is going to invite shame to stay a while. We cannot evolve into the person we are capable of being if we are held back by shame. On the flip side, when we view ourselves as good, our lights turn on. We will be empowered to step into a space with confidence.

This is the fun part. You are not stuck in your beliefs. Allow me to repeat with emphasis. YOU ARE NOT STUCK IN YOUR BELIEFS.

The unlearning process requires practice, but it can be done. The neural pathways in our brains are creatures of habit. Psychologist Deann Ware, Ph.D., explains that when brain cells communicate frequently, the connection between them strengthens, and "the messages that travel the same pathway in the brain over and over begin to transmit faster and faster."

Let's pretend you believe you are unlovable, but you want to believe you are lovable. If you constantly dwell on how unlovable you are (inaccurate), the neural pathways for that belief become stronger. But if you begin to consistently dwell on how lovable you are (accurate), the neural pathways for that belief become stronger. The more times a pathway is activated, inaccurate or accurate, the less effort it takes to be triggered. The pathways you create in your brain become your new normal and you believe you are lovable. (You are.)

Don't expect to swap a disempowered belief for an empowered one overnight. Especially if you have believed pessimistic things about yourself for lengthy periods of time. It takes effort and consistency to reprogram our brains, similar to working out. Do you know how if you haven't worked out in a while it takes a considerable amount of reps to obtain abs? You might not see a difference after day one or two or three. But if you continue to show up and put in the work, eventually, you'll start to see results. The exercise will not get easier, but you will get stronger. Just like building up muscle mass, we can discipline our minds to unlearn negative and limiting belief patterns.

Before we can restructure our brains to dwell on healthier beliefs, we must identify the root of our negative beliefs. Only after we pinpoint the habits we need to undo can we undo them. Calling out our blind spots is half the battle of recovery. So, if you can admit that you have some work to do, congratulations! You are now able to practice creating new neural pathways in your brain. Hooray! Let's train our brains to entertain beliefs that we want to actualize. Once you open up your heart to grow, the growth will come.

Sex Before Marriage

At age 11, barely old enough to shave my legs, my mom took me on a girls' trip with the intention of giving me *the talk*. I would have preferred a speedy lecture, like ripping off a Band-Aid. Instead, *the talk* was drawn out over the course of a mother-daughter weekend trip to Texas. Trapped in a tiny cabin on a dude ranch, Mom explained where babies come from. I got the lowdown on the logistics of sexual intercourse. In addition to the usual science stuff, I also received some bonus material.

Mom brought along a Christian-themed syllabus that relied on a manual on how God views sex plus five hours of tape recordings. I had the pleasure of listening to all five tapes on the "vacation." The narrators, who I'll refer to as Bernie and Denise, discuss the beauty of sex if—and only if—it's within the context of marriage. By marriage, Bernie and Denise meant marriage between a husband and a wife—and only a wife—if you catch my drift. More explicitly, homophobia was considered to be God-honoring.

I made my way through the lessons and learned how God desired for me at minimum to preserve my virginity for the night of my wedding. Lucky for me, the kit included props, which are now ingrained in my brain for all of eternity. Aside from a balloon and a banana, I can vividly recall one prop, in particular: a silk rose. The rose came in a Ziploc baggie along with its partnering reading material, a short story of a high school girl. Mom broke the seal and removed the rose from its confinement, and following instructions, she read the fictional tale aloud while holding up the rose, plucking its petals off one-by-one as the plot unfolded. It went something like this:

Emily was like a rose. Despite a few thorns here and there, she was beautiful. All of her rose petals were intact; she was whole. Yet, as she surrendered her heart and body to a boy, gradually, Emily's rose petals fell off. One after another, her petals dropped until only the stem remained.

At the beginning of her senior year, Emily developed a crush on a guy named Brad. Brad was very cute. Emily was shy; she had trouble mustering up the courage to talk to Brad. Instead, she dreamt about him, and she wrote her name with his name in her diary. Emily was crushing hard from a distance. Emily gave into her emotions. Rose petal. Pluck.

Emily wanted to get Brad's attention. She drove herself to the mall and shopped for something that would catch Brad's eye. Emily tried on a tight-fitting, low-cut top. The top showed a hint of cleavage. Just a hint could do the trick. Emily bought the shirt. Emily compromised her modesty. Rose petal. Pluck.

The deep-v worked, Brad took notice of Emily. The two seniors started chatting it up in the hallway. Their conversions were flowing. It was as if they'd known each other for years. But talking wasn't enough. One afternoon, in between classes, Brad reached for Emily's hand. She interlocked her fingers with his. Emily yielded her hands. Rose petal. Pluck.

Later into the school year, after a football game, Brad asked Emily to be his girlfriend. Thrilled, she said yes. The two touched lips. Emily relinquished her lips. Rose petal. Pluck.

Once Emily and Brad began full-on dating, things spiraled out of control. Under a set of bleachers, the couple advanced to second base. Rose petal. Pluck.

In a parked car, third base. Rose petal. Pluck.

Months go by. It was prom night. Emily is down to her last petal. The temptation to go all the way was at an all-

*time high. Emily and Brad could not resist. Home run.
Emily laid down her virginity. Rose petal. Pluck.*

*Post-graduation, the high school sweethearts attended
separate colleges in separate states. In the end, long-
distance didn't work out. Emily and Brad parted ways,
never to see each other again. Years passed and Emily met
her true love, Nathan. Alas, Emily had nothing left to
give her husband. Nathan never got to unwrap the gift of
his wife in purity. Emily had already given away her most
precious treasure, her virginity, to Brad. Emily is now but
a measly stem. She lost all of her rose petals.*

Cringe City. Just listening to the story made me feel like I'd
lost a petal of purity. I felt naughty and dirty staring at the small
pile of silk rose petals on the carpet. I didn't want to be a stem.

The weekend concluded with a contract signing as a symbol
of course completion. It was a covenant between Jesus and me,
promising him that I would save my rose petals for my future
husband. The kicker was I had to declare *in writing* the exact
number of petals I'd keep intact. My mom watched as I internally
debated how far I'd go before crossing The Line. In progressing
order, I could choose from the following: holding hands, side
hugs, frontal hugs, kissing on the cheek, kissing on the lips,
making out, groping, undressing, giving a hand job, giving a blow

job and sexual intercourse. I wasn't exactly in touch with my sexuality at 11. I circled "frontal hug" and signed my name at the bottom.

After that mother-daughter rendezvous, I internalized a paramount, sole mission: Save Virginity for Future Husband.

As you can imagine, I was terrified to death of ever having sex before marriage. I figured God would hate me if I did, and Bernie and Denise would *definitely* hate me. That getaway freaked me out to do anything at all whatsoever with boys, which was probably the point. I didn't want to mess up by messing around. The teachings scarred me for life, yes, but I did buy into the concept of purity—100 percent.

The idea of suppressing your sexual desires in the name of Jesus was promoted all around me. There were actual propaganda posters in church hangout spaces that read, "Modest Is Hottest," and "True Love Waits." I also had a handful of friends who went through similar purity retreats. Again, when your parents, pastors and friends proclaim the same message, you simply adopt it, no questions asked.

Even so, all those voices combined did not compare to the weight of the New Testament. The Bible was the heaviest influence on my decisions. In a letter to the Corinthians, Paul pleads for followers of Christ to "flee sexual immorality." I interpreted fleeing sexual immorality to mean steering clear from any remotely risqué acts outside of a heterosexual legal union. I listened to Paul's advice because I believed Paul's advice to be God's advice. And I trusted God. I was confident that any warning in Scripture was written to benefit me in the long run. I assumed if I obeyed the said warning, my future sex life would be enriched. I would be guaranteed stuff, like a bangin' wedding night, an orgasmic honeymoon and a lifetime of marital erotica.

In my sophomore year of high school, I thought I'd found The One. He was cute, funny and super-Christian. What more could a Southern girl ask for? What really turned me on, though, was his desire to wait until his wedding ceremony to have his first kiss *and* to say, "I love you." I'd met my match. We were boyfriend and girlfriend for over two years, and I was all in.

I'll have you know, 24 months of gazing into your boyfriend's eyes and saying, "I like you so much," gets dull. Don't tell Bernie and Denise, but we started holding hands (there goes a rose petal). We began to frontal hug for 90 seconds on average— another rose petal. And alas, there were two instances in our relationship when we gave each other kisses on the cheek. (I *broke* my covenant with Jesus.) My boyfriend felt *terrible* about it. *I* felt terrible about it. Our behavior got *so* sinful—the hand-holding, frontal hugging and cheek-kissing—that the dude broke up with me. He said he felt convicted that our relationship was not honoring God. And apparently, God told him to break up with me.

Even though he and I barely did anything sexual whatsoever, I came away from that relationship with emotional damage. I was overcome with shame because I thought I'd let my boyfriend—whom I loved—and God down. I slipped into a depression post-breakup. Part of me thought I deserved to feel depressed. The deep sadness and rejection I felt were the consequences of my actions. *I broke my covenant with Jesus.* I thought I'd done something wrong, so I deserved to be dumped.

Another part of me, however, was thoroughly confused. My high school bf and I weren't *that* bad, were we? I had truly tried my darndest to be *godly*. So why did I get burned in the end? I experienced a romance sans physical intimacy and it still harmed me. I missed out on two years of make-out sessions for nothing. I started to get suspicious about my belief in utter abstinence, but I had a mission to accomplish: Save Virginity for Future Husband.

Much later, cherry unpopped, I married the hunkiest man alive, aka Beau Blake. For our wedding night and honeymoon, my expectations were high as a friggin' skyscraper. In being so adamant about not having it, I put sex on a pedestal. I worshipped it. Yet when it came time to execute, I froze. For twelve years, I had trained myself to be petrified of men in the nude. Now, I had a sexy-ass, naked hubby caressing my boobs and all I wanted to do was recoil. Goodness gracious, I was not prepared for the shame of purity culture to follow me into my marriage. As a married woman, I *still* felt like I was doing something wrong. My fears did not subside like I thought they would. Once I could participate in God-approved sex, I could not get myself to enjoy it. *Years* into our marriage I struggled to shake the guilt.

I regretted saving my virginity for Beau. I wish I'd had the chance to get in touch with my sexuality as a single person instead of having to work through that within the context of marriage. It was a hurdle I would have had to face anyways, but it would have been nice to conquer the hurdle ahead of time. Because, to my horror, my husband reaped *negative* consequences from me saving my "treasure" for him. It wasn't fair for Beau to be blindsided with a spouse who wanted to crawl in a hole and die after we were intimate. He did not deserve a wife who clammed up in the bedroom.

I was perplexed. I so wanted to be a partner who was free to initiate spontaneous, hot sex. But it was so difficult for me to get there because I had trauma associated with it. If obeying God's

Word is what's best for me, why do I feel so crummy? This is not what I had in mind when I chose to live my life according to the truths of the Bible.

I decided to conduct an investigation. I spoke with many, many Conservative Christian couples who opened up to me about their experiences with chastity. What I discovered time after time was that a lot of these people were also dealing with the repercussions of being immersed in purity culture. Whether it was the disappointment that comes with unmet expectations or the debilitating shame, almost every person I talked to could relate to my situation. I got to thinking, how could sexual immorality be a sin when fleeing from sexual immorality is causing people so much harm?

I believed sex before marriage was wrong because that's what the Bible points towards. But my experience and my research were telling me a different narrative. I was confronted with the opportunity to formulate my own opinion on sex. Not what Paul thought about sex, what I thought about sex. I wondered if sex before marriage is simply a choice—with consequences—like most decisions in life. Maybe sex before marriage is not wrong, maybe sex before marriage is *smart*.

We've dug into core beliefs, but we have yet to scratch the surface of *smaller* beliefs. You and I hold thousands and thousands of smaller beliefs that run the gamut. A smaller belief could be something inconsequential, like your take on Botox, or more substantial, like your thoughts on Capitalism. Smaller beliefs are the values we cling to, or the assumptions and opinions we make about anything or anyone. These beliefs we carry encompass a vast scope. You could believe you do not like avocados. You could believe in a Roth IRA, a 401K, yoga or modern medicine. In enneagrams, horoscopes, Trump, Obama or abstinence. You get the picture.

In theory, we're not as attached to our smaller beliefs as we are to our core ones. We tend to hold them with a looser grip. And when we hold a belief with a loose grip, that belief is more likely to shapeshift organically as we evolve. Oftentimes, a smaller belief comes undone when we encounter opinions in contradiction to it. For example, when you were little, you might have believed chocolate milk comes from brown cows. If a peer told you chocolate milk actually comes from cocoa powder, merely being presented with contrasting information puts your chocolate milk-cow belief in jeopardy. Or, you might have believed that teachers lived at schools. If your teacher tells you they do not live at a school, all of a sudden, your teachers-live-at-schools belief has the potential to morph into something else entirely.

The most common way a smaller belief gets affected is when we experience firsthand incriminating evidence against that belief. Let's say you believe if you step on a crack, it will break your mother's back. If you step on a crack and it does not break your mother's back, you are likely to let go of that belief. Or let's say you believe if you swallow a watermelon seed, a watermelon will grow inside your tummy. If you swallow a watermelon seed and a watermelon did not grow inside your tummy, chances are you're going to let go of that belief too.

Like a rock, my smaller belief that sex before marriage was wrong was solid. The little inconsistencies I experienced were like splashes of water. At first, they did not make enough of a difference to soften it. But over time, the more contradictions I bumped into, the more the surface of my smaller belief smoothed.

In his study of cognitive behavior, Chilean philosopher Humberto Maturana concluded that all of our beliefs work in tandem to form a system. Since our core beliefs were formed first, we form our smaller beliefs through the lens of our core beliefs. I developed my belief in abstinence in the first place because of a core belief in the Bible as absolute Truth. I would never have died on a hill for my belief in abstinence. But I might have taken a bullet for my belief in the Bible being the absolute Truth.

In comparison to our core beliefs, smaller beliefs might not seem as important. But actually, they're kind of a big deal. Maturana found that because all beliefs are connected, a change in one belief enacts a chain reaction, a domino effect. Meaning that over time, if a smaller belief is affected, it can bring down a core belief. And if a core belief is affected, it can ultimately lead to the disruption of the system as a whole.

Permission Slip

I do not remember making a conscious decision to be a Dallas Cowboys fan. My dad and brother, Jack, rooted for the Cowboys, so I rooted for the Cowboys. If I had given my allegiance more thought, really any thought at all, I would not have chosen the excruciating heartache involved with being a part of the Cowboys' fan base. We're talking loss after loss after loss. After loss.

Each year when fall rolled around, Dad, Jack and I bonded over our sports-related woes. In one game in particular, the Cowboys were facing 4th-and-2 on the 32-yard line and decided to go for it. All we needed was a touchdown to pull ahead of our arch-nemesis, the Green Bay Packers. With four minutes and 42 seconds remaining in the fourth quarter, quarterback Tony Romo lobbed the football to wide receiver Dez Bryant and Bryant caught it just short of the end zone, inside the one-yard line. Standing on seats in the living room, the three of us whooped and hollered in sheer glee—until the officiating crew ruled it as a non-catch. And just like that, we lost the game. What did I tell you? Heartache.

You may not be attached to the Cowboys but my guess is there is a team or athlete you are a fan of. Most of us find ourselves connected to a specific team or athlete because of the family or city we were born into. I don't know about you, but if I were to tell my brother I converted to a Packers fan it wouldn't bode well for me on Thanksgiving. Or worse, if I were to give up watching football entirely he might not ever speak to me again. For that very reason, I plan on supporting the Cowboys and football for the rest of my life.

Imagine if we took a step back to analyze the data around professional football. Let's say we researched each NFL team's stats in order to land on an informed decision. That way, rather than blind loyalty, we could consciously choose which team we wanted to support. My guess is if we went off wins and losses, no one would be a Cowboys fan.

Environmentally-influenced fandom works because it's just for fun. I mean, family camaraderie is great, and cheering for a team in close proximity to where you live makes sense as it's easier to attend a game in person. Yet so often, we absorb our beliefs like we absorb a football team. I think we can all agree our beliefs are not a game and deserve to be taken seriously. If what we believe shapes how we view ourselves, others and the world, wouldn't we want to explore all possibilities in order to see if a better, more pleasant view exists?

It takes guts to unlearn beliefs and entertain new ones. Consider this chapter your permission slip. I've signed my name at the bottom. No need to turn it in, this is just for you. I extend you my full permission to navigate uncharted regions. You can root for another football team, practice another religion, or vote for another candidate. You can ask questions. If you have to disagree with yourself, so be it. If you have to leave your friends and family behind, so be it. You can be your own person, you can be *unique*. Your decisions, opinions, actions, words, *beliefs*, are all yours. You can be you.

Beau and I agree on most things, but our views are vastly different on how to spend a Saturday. For Beau, Saturdays are for winding down from the week prior. It's a day to kick up his feet, play some video games and watch a movie. For me, a Saturday is about getting shit done. All of the tasks I do not otherwise have time to complete, I complete on Saturday. Wiping down the baseboards, getting the oil changed or organizing the storage closet. It must be thoroughly enjoyable to be married to one of us…

The storage closet in our apartment is where we store things like our vacuum, sports equipment and random crap. It's a frightening place. I make a point to reorganize it every few months (on Saturday) or else it gets out of hand. I'll admit that when I deep clean the storage closet, it looks like I'm dirtying instead of cleaning; my go-to method is to remove every item from the closet and set it in the hallway.

I sort everything into two piles: keep or toss. The throw out pile never fails to surprise me. I usually end up staring at it in disbelief. I think, "Why on earth did I decide to keep this piece of junk?" Only a few months before, I'd taken every single thing out of that closet in order to examine which pile I should assign it to. And the last time I decluttered I decided to put an empty bottle of Advil back in its place on a shelf...?

The last time I decluttered, I was able to recognize what I couldn't see the time I decluttered before—I was storing items that were no longer serving a purpose.

We must go through a similar process in order to analyze our beliefs. If we want to continue growing, we have to identify what beliefs we are holding onto that are no longer serving a purpose. We have to dump all of our beliefs on the floor and sort them into piles. Keep or unlearn?

It's important to note that this is not a one-and-done kind of thing; it's an exercise we must take part in regularly. The first time around we might not be in the space to discern which beliefs need to be scratched and which ones need to stay. Or the second time around. Or the third. It's an every-few-months type of process. (Think about it: if we did select our football teams based on statistics, the team we would pick to win the Super Bowl would vary year to year. Probably depending on whichever team Tom Brady is on.)

Taking everything out and setting it in the "hallway" is the first step to deconstructing your beliefs. Who knows, you might want to put all of your beliefs back in their place. Or maybe you'll want to toss them all out and start over. Or maybe it's somewhere in between. In any case, I must warn you: it gets messier before it gets tidier.

Disneyland

If you're in the 99.9th percentile of the earth's population, you've most likely never been to Little Rock, Arkansas. It's beautiful. It's full of forests and lakes. There's summer, winter, spring, and fall. There are chain restaurants and cookie-cutter houses and parking lots half a mile long. Unbeknownst to my childhood self, being raised in Little Rock, I was encircled by my own kind: white, wealthy, straight, Republican Christians.

Los Angeles is like Disneyland. It's an amusement park where every gender, sexual orientation, religion, race and economic class imaginable is represented. You will bump elbows with Armenians and Arkansans, drag queens and Episcopalians. You'll be on a rollercoaster seated next to an unhoused woman on your left and Jake Gyllenhaal on your right. All variations of humans coexisting in a land of entertainment and overpriced food.

Like new butterflies, Beau and I moved to Los Angeles and shed the layers of our environmental cocoons. We entered a realm of newness. Everything was new—the people, culture, food, weather, politics, etc. It was quite a culture shock. For starters, I relocated from a conservative neighborhood to a liberal neighborhood. Not only did I relocate from a conservative neighborhood to a liberal neighborhood, I relocated from a conservative neighborhood to a liberal neighborhood during a presidential election. Not just any ol' presidential election, I relocated from a conservative neighborhood to a liberal neighborhood during one of the most controversial presidential elections in American history: Donald Trump vs Hillary Clinton.

By spending most of my existence in the Bible Belt, I was taught both indirectly and directly that the godly ballot is a Republican ballot. Jesus would vote Republican and Jesus would vote for Trump. In Little Rock, almost none of my beliefs were challenged. In fact, they were reinforced. Everywhere I went and everyone I talked to confirmed what I thought I already knew. My family, my friends, their friends, my church, the radio, Facebook timeline and Instagram feed all espoused what I believed. I'd built my life around the opposite of newness: sameness.

A good percentage of my Southern friends were supportive of our move to Cali, with the exception of a few who expressed their concerns. I got the usual, "But the traffic," and "It's so expensive," mostly from people who had not once stepped foot in LA. The number one pushback I got, however, was along the lines of "The Liberals." One relative, in all seriousness, said, "Promise me you will not go to the dark side," i.e. make a promise that I would not become a Democrat. In all earnestness, I replied, "I promise." I planned on standing my ground as a right-wing Christian for as long as I lived. I'd be the solo Conservative in the state if that's what it came down to. Sameness.

I felt a supernatural calling to the West Coast. In the deepest parts of me, I knew I had to answer the call. It didn't take long for Los Angeles to move me. The lights, the billboards, the people, the fashion, the *energy*... I was home. LA allowed me to take a giant exhale as if I'd been holding my breath for years. Although I did not know exactly what I was getting myself into at the time, I did know from the get-go that I belonged. And that confused me. Big time. I went into the transition with my walls of cement UP, especially against those damn Liberals. I thought, how come, immersed in such a progressive atmosphere, I felt so... light? Isn't light good?

The initial impact of the city was strong enough to take down a few of my defenses, but many remained. I tried my damndest to stay stubborn and unswayed. I reminded myself over and over of who I was: a child of God. And a child of God is a white, wealthy, straight, Republican Christian. Right?

I'd heard about liberal churches in California, the kinds that do not stick to the Scriptures. More specifically, the pastors at these particular churches preach—as Fundamentalists call it—a "watered-down gospel." This means the sermons given from the pulpit are "all about love," and are lacking in "truth" also known as judgment. You'd think declaring a message all about love would be good…?

So, when Beau and I found a Cali church we liked, I was hesitant to join. I needed to make sure this church was legit and *not* watered down. Before agreeing to become members, I requested a meeting with a deacon of the church to solidify that it checked all of my boxes. I asked the deacon for a copy of their bylaws to examine if the church's beliefs aligned with mine. Would they marry someone who had sex before marriage? Would they marry a gay couple? Would they tolerate drunkenness? Would they allow a woman to be a pastor? Because the deacon answered no to all of my inquisitions, I made the decision to join.

Recalling this, my cheeks flush with embarrassment. *wince*

Beau and I might have found the single most legalistic church in LA. Regardless, we found a magnificent community of friends there. The congregation made us feel at ease in the vastness of the city. To find people who believed the same things we believed in regards to faith made us *comfortable*.

As we got to know the church peeps on a deeper level, we conversed openly about stuff like aspirations, vulnerabilities and politics. Through conversation after conversation, Beau and I started putting two and two together that our new friends, our new *Christian* friends, were all planning to vote for Hillary. Wait, what? That was *not* comfortable.

It didn't surprise me that California is so Democratic-leaning it's basically a blueberry. I knew this going in. What I didn't realize, however, was so many of those Democrats were also Christians. The fact that an individual could believe in the Resurrection, the Trinity, the Scriptures and vote for a candidate who is (a) a woman and (b) pro-LGBTQ+ and (c) pro-choice did not compute. It felt blasphemous.

Around the same time as this discovery, one of my closest friends from my alma mater, the University of Arkansas, brought her boyfriend to visit. While giving a brief tour of Rodeo Drive, I shared how I was feeling confused politically. My Christian friends from the South believed Jesus would vote for Trump, and my Christian friends in Los Angeles believed Jesus would vote for Clinton. My friend's boyfriend said, "All I know is you are not a true Christian if you vote for Hillary."

I used to think that too, man. But my new California besties were definitely Christians. Something didn't add up. Both parties backed up their stances with Scripture to support their case. How is it that both groups are drawing from the exact same text and landing on completely different conclusions? Which side is right?

We can't all be right, right?

For months, I attempted to untangle this political web, scrutinizing each issue with a Biblical lens. It's a miracle my brain did not erupt from the sheer bamboozlement of the back and forth. To my genuine surprise, I found substantial arguments in the Bible to back up each issue on each side. There are plenty of verses, not taken out of context, that support the ideas of those who are pro-choice. There are plenty of verses, not taken out of context, that supports the ideas of those who are pro-life. The same goes for economical stances, opinions on guns, gay people, women in leadership, Socialism, Capitalism, social justice, gender equality and more.

I wanted to find evidence that a woman should not be president and I found it in the Bible. I wanted to find evidence that a woman should be president and I found it in the Bible. If the words in the Bible are God's words, and the words in the Bible can be interpreted in contrasting ways, who does God actually want me to vote for? Is Jesus a Republican? Or is Jesus a Democrat? Either way, how can I know for sure?

I realized that both groups, Conservative Christians and Progressive Christians, were picking and choosing the verses in the Word of God that aligned with their desired political take. *Both groups were interpreting the Bible through the lens of their already formed beliefs.* As was I.

Fun fact: it is documented in the Bible that Jesus is asked 183 questions. Guess how many he answers? Three. Three! Clearly, Jesus is not in the business of dishing out answers.

I was after answers, but I bumped up against something better: the freedom to decide for myself. I do not know who Jesus would vote for because I am not Jesus. I let go of trying to guess what Jesus would want me to do and took back responsibility for my personal growth. And dare I say, maybe, that's exactly what Jesus would want me to do.

My existing political beliefs, the totality of what I had known to be true, encountered a crossroads. I could either hang on for dear life to my old values or dip my toe into a sea of the unknown. Sameness or newness?

Conservative Christian or Progressive Christian?

Sarah Girouard or Sarah Blake?

The Golden Staircase

It makes sense why many newlyweds spend their honeymoon at an all-inclusive resort. When the only things on the agenda are lounging beachside and nursing prepaid margaritas, there's not much to argue about. Against all wisdom, Beau and I decided to put our newfound matrimony to the test with our honeymoon destination. The two of us went on a 211-mile backpacking trip.

Beau and I hiked California's John Muir Trail (JMT). North to south, the trail begins in Yosemite Valley and ends on top of a fourteener called Mt. Whitney. It took us 18 days to complete. That's an average of walking one half-marathon per day, which would be a feat on flat ground, but we walked one half-marathon per day across mountain passes of ungodly elevation gains while carrying 35-pound packs on our backs. It was basically pure torture apart from the breathtaking views. The worst part, though, was knowing we could give up at any moment. And on day 11, I almost did.

Like any other morning on the hike, I awoke and laid in my warm, cozy sleeping bag until I thought my bladder might explode. I got up begrudgingly and found a semi-secluded place in the snow to squat and pee. Beau and I ate granola bars for breakfast for the 11th day in a row. The two of us collapsed our tent, rolled up our "beds" and stuffed the rest of the belongings in our packs. I pulled out the map to check out our itinerary before venturing out. The next campsite on our schedule was eight miles away, just over a mountain called The Golden Staircase. Wonderful.

The Golden Staircase is misery in the form of an incline. We hit the foot of it when we hit mile seven, and after that, it's literally an entire mile of steps. The gradient was so steep we couldn't see where the steps ended. While ascending, I think I told Beau I wanted to give up at least 30 times. (As I said, we put our marriage to the test.) I thought my legs were going to fall off. The only hope keeping me moving was that if I just made it to the top, we could set up camp and I could get back in my sleeping bag.

After pep talks from Beau and a few tears from me, we summited The Golden Staircase. We enjoyed our victory for about two seconds because we could now see what we couldn't before: Mather Pass. Frantically, I got out the map, and to my absolute dismay, I saw that I had misread it. The next campsite was not just over The Golden Staircase, it was just over Mather

Pass, another six miles away. I thought we had arrived but we weren't even close. We had yet another mountain range to conquer before the sun went down.

The good news is that eventually we made it to our campsite on day 11 and summited Mt. Whitney on day 18, and almost five years later Beau and I are still very much in love. If I could go back and alter my perspective during that arduous trip, I would choose to enjoy the exploration instead of gunning for the destination. Hiking the John Muir Trail was meant to be an in-the-moment adventure. It was not about arriving at the end, it was about soaking up the scenery along the way. Nevertheless, if you see my husband please let him know that I am not opposed to hitting up an all-inclusive for our next anniversary. I'll take some mezcal and ocean views, please.

A couple summers ago, I watched Spike Lee's film *BlacKkKlansman* on a plane ride from LA to Dallas. I tossed my AWAY suitcase into the overhead bin and settled in for the 2.5-hour flight. It's the perfect amount of time to watch a movie in its entirety. Usually I try to keep it PG on planes out of consideration for my fellow passengers, but this time I deviated from my own ritual and I'm glad I did.

If you haven't seen it, *BlacKkKlansman* is based on a true story. In summary, a Black detective named Ron Stallworth infiltrates the Colorado Springs Ku Klux Klan in order to investigate the illegal activity of its members. Stallworth develops a relationship via phone with David Duke, a grand wizard of the Knights of the KKK. During their phone conversations, Stallworth convinces Duke that he loathes both Black and Jewish people, and Duke signs Stallworth's Klan certificate of membership. In real life and in the movie, in 1970 Ron Stallworth became the KKK's only Black member.

In addition to the flight turbulence, *BlacKkKlansman* made me sick to my stomach. Throughout the movie, the white supremacist group said and did horrendous things. To a millennial like me, the 1970s seems like a long time ago, so I found some relief in the fact that the movie did not take place in our modern day. But the most horrific scenes came just before the credits.

In these scenes, Spike Lee reveals actual footage from 2017 of Duke and his politically active followers. The clip shows Duke at a white supremacist rally, encouraging folks to support Donald Trump. Duke is in his 70s and still kicking it. And he *still* has the backing of a considerable number of people who align with his beliefs.

I turned off the screen, took a bite of a Biscoff cookie, and sank into my seat. I was utterly perplexed. The reality of 21st century KKK members and white supremacists hit me hard. Mind spinning and my heart in turmoil, I got the bad type of chills. *How the heck do people believe this stuff?*

The movie got me thinking: how wild is it that the KKK, Neo-Nazis, Scientologists, Satanists, *terrorists*, think their beliefs are right? There are members of extremist groups who are willing to die for their beliefs, and that is not an exaggeration. And, there are members of extremist groups who are willing to discriminate, oppress and *kill* for the sake of living out their "truths." Most of these organizations and individuals wholeheartedly believe their conclusions to be correct when their conclusions are clearly delusional. It's bizarre and a little scary.

Do you know what else is wild? Fundamentalists, Catholics, Lutherans, Hindus, Jews, Buddhists, Mormons, Muslims, Atheists, Conservatives and Liberals, think their beliefs are right, too. It's kind of awkward if you think about it. Which group is right?

We can't all be right, right?

I used to treat my beliefs—spiritual, political, cultural—like an end goal I could reach. More accurately, I used to treat my beliefs like I had already arrived at the final destination. I thought I could set up camp and make my bed where I was, but I wasn't where I thought I was. Rather than opening my heart to explore a variety of truths and possibilities, I was stuck. Stuck in my beliefs at the near-beginning of life's journey—age 25. I had every intention of believing what I believed at age 25 forever and ever. If I am honest with myself, I was so certain of this because I thought I was right. Which, if you think about it, automatically labels anyone who disagrees with me as wrong.

Thinking I'd arrived in my beliefs resulted in me becoming insufferably arrogant, much like I'd imagine extremists to be. Yuck. Arrogance closed me off to openness. Instead, I clenched my fists because I was so sure that I was right even when my beliefs were hurting me. I couldn't see it from where I was standing, but there was yet another mountain to climb. And another mountain to climb after that and another mountain to climb and after that times infinity.

The thing is that when we hold problematic beliefs, we are completely and utterly *oblivious* to the problem. We all have blind spots. Failing to push past the boundaries of what you know to be true in the present is a recipe for rightness. Rightness is camouflaged arrogance. And arrogance is spreading from one adult to another like the coronavirus. We must routinely ask ourselves, "What am I not seeing?"

Socrates said, "The only true wisdom consists in knowing that you know nothing." Socrates also said, "There is only one good, knowledge, and one evil, ignorance." If you think about it, these two statements appear to be contradictory. It is my interpretation that in the first saying he is humbly admitting that, despite all his education, he does not have life figured out. In the other, he advocates for the importance of acquiring knowledge. Furthermore, Socrates stresses the ethical responsibility of gaining understanding.

I think Socrates is on to something. Knowing that we don't know is just as vital as actively seeking out what we don't know. It's both-and. For that reason, it is imperative to recognize that our beliefs have not and will not reach any sort of terminus. If we want to access life's fullest, dreamiest potential, we must hold our perspectives loosely, continually exploring—and being open to—other perspectives as well. Because, like Socrates hints in the second quote, the consequences of ignorance can be ruinous. Thinking we know it all stunts our personal growth. And we could be bringing adversity unknowingly to ourselves or others by simply sticking to some beliefs without question for long periods of time. If this is possible, wouldn't it be our moral obligation to unlearn those beliefs?

Psychologist and TED speaker Adam Grant introduced me to the idea of keeping an "ignorance list".[v] Grant believes we are all capable of making lists of things we know absolutely nothing about. So, just when I start to feel like I have arrived or like I have life nailed, I intentionally remind myself to attempt to know that I do not know. In other words, I call out and highlight my own ignorance on a regular basis. Here's my latest list:

I do not know much about David Bowie.

I do not know much about nuclear weapons.

I could not tell you one thing about land lobsters, except that they're a type of insect.

I could not tell you one thing about the movie *Casablanca*, but I hear it's good.

I pretend to know everything about politics and religion. I definitely do not.

I pretend to know everything about me. I definitely do not.

What are you ignorant about?

Our reality is one of forever exploration and endless expansion. Life is not about arriving, it's about exploring. Life is not about answers, it's about the search. Life is not about being right, it's about being *open*. How can one be right about life? Let's lean into the friction and take in the views along the way. Let's attempt to know that we don't know.

Accutane

I worked for a skincare brand for nearly three years. Back when I joined, I was their 10th employee, and the company was still very much a start-up. From conception, the company made a commitment to formulate its beauty products with clean ingredients. It's a miracle I was hired because my knowledge of the skincare industry, and skincare in general, was zilch. I am grateful that I was introduced to the clean beauty movement through my time as an employee.

You remember when my face was freaking out because my hormones were out of whack? Before my friend Katie gently guided me to that diagnosis, I sought professional help. I paid a visit to my dermatologist's office in Beverly Hills. I asked my dermatologist what I needed to do to heal my skin. To my bewilderment, she recommended Accutane as a fix right off the bat. *Accutane?*

In working for the skincare company, I was made aware of Accutane's potential side effects. Thankfully. Call me crazy, but I was not interested in using a product that has been linked to birth defects, IBS and increased rates of suicide. I probably would not have thought twice about questioning the dermatologist's recommendation if I had not been employed at such a cutting-edge beauty brand. Frankly, the old me would have taken her advice, no questions asked. Merely by surrounding myself with holistically-minded co-workers, I couldn't help but learn more about the clean beauty movement. I turned myself into a conscious consumer.

With the Internet at our fingertips, consumers in today's world are more educated than in years past. A report published by the Statista Research Department in 2019 revealed that more than 50 percent of Americans look for organic or natural products when shopping for cosmetics. Rather than blindly purchasing products, beauty kings and queens are now checking product labels for harmful ingredients such as parabens. (The FDA acknowledges several studies linking parabens to breast cancer, skin cancer, and decreased sperm count.)

If I may be so bold as to guess her age, I estimate my dermatologist obtained her college degree about 25 years ago. A lot has changed since she and many other practicing skincare professionals were in undergrad. For starters, 25 years ago the FDA had not publicly announced the harmful effects of parabens. Or Accutane. I wonder: how many other dermatologists are basing their prescriptions on outdated information?

To put this in perspective, about 25 years ago, in 1992, the USDA Food Guide Pyramid was broadcast to Americans with bread and pasta making up the largest portion of the pyramid. As continued research chipped away at the healthy eating recommendations, within just a few years, the pyramid was modified to deduct refined carbohydrates and re-released in 2005. In 2011, after more research, the USDA replaced the pyramid completely with MyPlate, which promotes a more balanced consumption of grains, fruits, vegetables, protein and dairy. I wonder how many Americans have not received the latest memo? I wonder how many Americans are still basing their well-intended meals off the original Food Guide Pyramid?

Knowledge is evolving. Due to advances in technology, astronomers now know that Pluto is not a planet. Due to prior limited research, experts used to think it was okay to place children in the backseat of a car, unbuckled. Failing to get up to speed with the most recent data could be causing more damage than good. If we remain ignorant to the newest-of-the-new information, our beliefs could be misinformed because our knowledge—however limited—informs our beliefs.

Let's take seat belts for instance. Knowing the facts around seat belts shapes your belief with regard to whether you think it's important to wear a seat belt or not. What if you read that according to the National Highway Traffic Safety Association, of the 37,133 people killed in motor vehicle crashes in 2017, 47 percent were not wearing seat belts? Or what if you discovered that in 2017 alone, seat belts saved an estimated 14,955 lives and *could have* saved an additional 2,549 people if they had been wearing seat belts? After exposing yourself to those data points, you are probably going to believe it's important to wear a seat belt. And if you wear a seat belt, it could save your life. If you don't, it could kill you.

Not to be too dramatic, but real talk: informed beliefs can be a matter of life or death. I'm not saying that we have to accept all novel information as truth. Still, I am advocating for intentionally seeking out information and ideas that are different from what we already know. Of course, we can make the decision if we want to take on the opposing stance or not. But what we don't want to do is instantly shut it down. It's useless to seek out other opinions and look into other perspectives if we're not open to entertaining them.

Beliefs, like knowledge, are meant to evolve. Yet like sap on a tree, our understanding solidifies into a resin as we grow older.

Endemic to the human experience is a perceived cap on our growth—and rigidity around our beliefs is to blame. It's like we hit the pause button on learning. If we do not evolve our knowledge, we are unlikely to evolve our beliefs. If we do not evolve our beliefs, we are less likely to flourish.

Think about what you believed when you were four years old. Did you have an imaginary friend? Did you believe in Santa? Let's face it, it'd be concerning if you still believed in imaginary friends and Santa Claus. Likewise, it'd be concerning if, when you turn 84, you still believe the things you believed when you were 34. No matter if we are four, 34 or 84, we have not yet arrived—and it is *awesome*.

Two Birthdays

I have two birthdays. February 23rd—the day I was physically brought into this world—and January 7th.

On January 7th, 1998, at age four, I prayed a prayer that would get me into heaven (as told by my parents). That morning, my mom's best friend, Mrs. Jennifer, passed away from breast cancer. I was curious as to where she'd gone. Piglet jammies on, I climbed into my parents' bed. I asked Mom and Dad what had happened to Mrs. Jennifer. According to them, because Mrs. Jennifer had Jesus in her heart, she went to live in heaven.

In heaven, the streets are paved with gold. Heaven is where dogs and cats go after they die. Gold streets and puppies? Sign me up. In the company of my parents, I prayed to ask Jesus to live in my heart. Dad said to repeat after him: "Jesus, I invite you to live in my heart." (Jesus, I invite you to live in my heart.)

Boom. Done. That's it. Everlasting life was so easy a four-year-old could do it. Afterward, my dad made me a plaque, like a trophy, that read the date and *Sarah's Born-again Birthday*.

Two birthdays.

To commemorate my salvation, my parents let me pick out a treat at Lifeway Christian Bookstore every born-again birthday. I took my pick of engraved journals, WWJD bracelets and Left Behind books (a fictional series about the rapture and the end times). I numbered myself both in biological years and in Christian years. Six years a human, two years a Christian and so on.

In first grade, I played point guard on an Upward basketball team. The Upward organization, a little league for elementary-aged Christians, would appoint one of their adult staff members to share the gospel of Jesus during half-time. At the end of each gospel presentation, the speaker would offer up an invitation for folks in the bleachers to invite Jesus to move into their hearts, too. That person would ask the crowd to say The Prayer ("Jesus, I invite you to live in my heart") silently to themselves.

I distinctly remember feeling pretty darn special when I heard one of those talks. Clearly, reciting The Prayer was imperative. It was a golden ticket into heaven and I had already secured mine. Many, many others in the world—adults included—had not yet taken this rudimentary step to ensure them an eternal fate of paradise. Gold streets and puppies! Yet here I was, a first-grader, who was light-years ahead of the rest of the universe. I tuned out the half-time talks because I didn't need to say the prayer *again*, it was a one-and-done kind of thing. I was covered. I was exceptional.

Before I asked Jesus to live in my heart, I was dead, a zombie. The church based this doctrine on a verse from the New Testament: "God, who is rich in mercy, made us alive with Christ even when we were dead in transgressions—it is by grace you have been saved." (Eph. 2.5 NIV) So, after I asked Jesus to live in my heart, I was alive.

It was called a Born-again Birthday because from ages 0 to 4, I was nomming, napping, spitting up, peeing, pooping, crawling and toddling around *dead*. Dead in my toddler transgressions. But as soon as I muttered the right ten words aloud, my afterlife fate was altered—and not a moment before.

I started labeling living, breathing humans as dead or alive. Any human who had not prayed The Prayer was dead with a pulse. And after their hearts stop beating, they sure as hell were not going to heaven.

From my point of view, the dead people (non-Christians) were *projects*. I was taught that it was impossible for a person who did not "have" Jesus to experience true peace. Jesus was the answer to a life of fulfillment. Therefore, a person who did not "have" Jesus was not experiencing genuine joy. Even if a person appeared to be super content, well, deep down, I believed they weren't. Because real satisfaction was considered to be impossible without Jesus.

With that in mind, I took it upon myself to try and convince the dead people that they were dead. How exactly did I go about doing that, you ask? My scheme was simple. I would demonstrate just how alive I was as a result of being a Christian. After they witnessed my irresistible beam of light, they'd have an epiphany that they were missing something crucial (Jesus). If they noticed how supernaturally happy I was, they'd want a sip of the Kool-Aid. The idea was that they'd come to the realization that I was full and they were empty. I had the Truth and they did not.

Dead people were a scarcity in Little Rock, Arkansas. Besides my sixth-grade teacher, who was Muslim, and one Catholic neighbor, most everyone I knew had already prayed The Prayer. (Catholics aren't *real* Christians; in Fundamentalism, praying to Mary is blasphemy because Mary is not Jesus.) But in Los Angeles, I met many, many dead people. More accurately, I *befriended* many, many dead people.

During my second year in LA, I landed a job as an office manager for a fashion brand. The office space, my-coworkers and bosses looked like a scene straight out of *Devil Wears Prada*. The workplace took up the entire seventh floor of a design center in West Hollywood. A wraparound patio deck overlooked the city and supplied the best sunset views.

The outfits the women wore looked like what you would see in *Vogue* magazine. My colleagues strutted their stuff down the hallways as if they were walking on red carpets. I was equally impressed and intimidated. I felt like Anne Hathaway pre-makeover compared to my coworkers. The whole operation was glamorous. Except... for my role.

Instead of supporting one high-up fashionista akin to Meryl Streep's character, I granted the wishes of the entire office of 200+ people. My day-to-day duties were very assistant-esque. The company offered unlimited varied snacks and full-on catered meals and I had the pleasure of coordinating those perks. I manned the front desk, delivered packages, purchased groceries, contacted maintenance, restocked the kitchens, etc.

Restocking the kitchen was most involved. I'd load up a utility cart with coffee grounds, olive oil, yogurt, string cheese, paper plates, paper cups, paper towels, Hippeas, Kettle chips, chocolate bars, and roll it to the kitchen past desks that might as well have belonged to Emily Blunt. This ritual took me over an hour daily. The bonus? The ability to eavesdrop.

This goes without saying, but unlike in Arkansas, it's not cool to be a Christian in Los Angeles. Aside from the Jesus-lovers I met at my traditional church, I didn't know many *alive* folks in the city. When I met one in the wild it was like I'd spotted a rare and endangered species. So, when I discovered via Instagram that one of my trendy co-workers, Natalia, was a Christian, I was stoked.

Christians have a secret language: Christianese. If an individual shares a story of themselves reading their Bible, captions a photo with a verse, screenshots a worship song off Spotify or tags their location at a church, that's Christianese for, "I am a Christian." Natalia checked herself into Church Home (yes, Justin Bieber's church), and that's when I knew she was the real deal. Natalia was *alive*.

Natalia and I became fast friends. We talked about boys, fashion and God. As I got to know her well, I noticed something very different about how Natalia lived out her faith. Natalia loved all of her friends, believers and non-believers, with no hidden agenda. She enjoyed hanging with the dead people just as much as she enjoyed hanging with the alive people. To Natalia, the dead people were not projects. They were humans.

Furthermore, she wasn't trying to *convert* the dead people. Natalia treated her non-Christian friends like her actual friends. From observing her interactions with our coworkers, I could tell that she wasn't trying to convince them to change. Natalia wasn't secretly leading those people to say The Prayer. She wasn't on a covert operation to show them just how empty they were and how fulfilled she was. Natalia treated them as *equals*. Natalia loved her friends just as they were. Go figure.

Her behavior gave me pause. It's not that I didn't have non-believing friends. I did. It's just that if I befriended a person who was not a Christian, I couldn't relax. I felt it was my responsibility to be the light of Jesus in their life—be extra kind, avoid gossip, invite them to church, talk about God, yadda yadda. My guard was up. My walls were up. I had to perform. It appeared like I was a good friend from the outside, but in reality, I had a hidden agenda: Convert Non-Christians to Christianity.

Convert the Dead People to Be Like Me!

One morning at work, I stood on a chair in my Zara heels to pour the coffee grinds into the giant coffee machine in the kitchen. Natalia (alive) walked in with her guy friend slash co-worker (dead). The two of them were in mid-conversation. From the snippets I heard, it sounded like her friend was describing a date he went on with another man. I took my time restocking to listen in. Natalia's friend said he *really* liked the guy he went out with. And at the end of his story, he told Natalia that the dude asked him to be his boyfriend. A gay relationship...

I leaned in, curious as to how Natalia would react.

To my shock, Natalia let out a gleeful gasp. Immediately, without hesitation, Natalia flung up her arms and embraced her friend in a full-on, swaying-back-and-forth-jumping-up-and-down bear hug.

I was dumbfounded.

I couldn't get behind Natalia's response because I was tethered to the Bible. The New Testament clearly addresses homosexuality as a sinful lifestyle. In Paul's letter to the Corinthians, he writes:

> Do you not know that wrongdoers will not inherit the kingdom of God? Do not be deceived: Neither the sexually immoral nor idolaters nor adulterers nor men who have sex with men nor thieves nor the greedy nor drunkards nor slanderers nor swindlers will inherit the kingdom of God. (1 Cor 6.9-10 NIV)

You know the drill: to me, Paul's words equaled God's words. If Paul said men who have sex with men are wrongdoers, shouldn't we Christians *not* be celebrating sinful behavior? How could we condone a sin?

Before I befriended Natalia, I had lived by the phrase, "Hate the sin, love the sinner." To be honest, I thought that was a great M.O. to live by because even though I viewed gay people, Jews,

Hindus, Buddhists, Muslims, Mormons and so on as sinners, I could still love them. What differentiated my approach from Natalia's was the "love" I gave, which was tainted with judgment. Hers was not. And in my current opinion, love tainted by judgment is not really love at all. It's self-righteousness.

Natalia did not view homosexuality as a sin. Therefore, she was able to love her gay friend without silently wanting him to change his lifestyle. As long as I viewed a gay person's lifestyle as *wrong*, and "dead" people in general as *wrong*, my love for those individuals would be capped. I could not freely celebrate my non-Christian friend's wins while I viewed their wins as sins. I could not freely grieve their sorrows while I viewed their sorrows as I-told-you-sos.

Natalia was free. Her friend was free. I was restricted. I was chained to the literal interpretation of Scripture.

Beneath the surface of my heart, deep, deep down, Natalia's approach to life resonated. Under the thick layers of my environment and through the walls I'd built, the truth that love is love resonated in my soul. The real truth.

I rode my bike home from work that day in a funk. Natalia's reaction to her friend's news, and the ease with which she loved others, wholly wrecked me. The simplicity of celebrating love in any form was something I did not have. I wanted it. I needed it.

I'll never forget being lost in my thoughts at a stoplight. Then and there I resolved to take ownership of my life and how it affects others. I made a conscious decision to take responsibility for my beliefs and actions. I chose to love people, all people, without judgment. No more performances. No more hidden agendas.

The more I practiced loving people for the sake of loving people, I realized that so many people who I thought needed changing did not in fact need changing. I took a hammer to my walls and let non-Christian friends into my inner circle. I got close with humans who were different from me.

I developed strong connections with couples in loving, committed, gay relationships. I couldn't help but notice most of those friends were genuinely full of abundant life. None of them had prayed The Prayer, and yet I witnessed true peace and hope and love in their lives. The more I hung out with dead people, the more I realized they were not dead. They were alive.

Netflix's *Queer Eye* is such a good example of this. If you have not seen *Queer Eye*, I cannot recommend it enough. It is undeniable that the men in that show are some of the kindest, most genuine, brightest lights on this planet. The Fab Five are true to themselves. The Five live life unchained and can love with no strings attached. By befriending queer folks and watching episode after episode of *Queer Eye*, I came to realize that I was the one in need of the gospel; Natalia and my "dead" friends had what I did not: freedom. *They* were sharing the gospel with *me*.

I noticed a pattern: the people who were true to themselves were the people who were alive. I was not. I was in a coma. Semi-dead.

If an LBGTQ+ human finds utter joy in doing *the exact opposite* of what Paul says, why in the heck would I agree with Paul's words? Why would God agree with Paul's words?

Gradually, like the slow force of water dripping continuously on a rock, my belief in homosexuality as a sin eroded.

It's not my fault I was born into a legalistic, rigid set of doctrines. But as a fully functioning adult, I can no longer hide behind the guise of ignorance. It is my moral obligation to look into all of my beliefs and why I believe them. I owe it to my personal growth and to evolution to open up my heart and unleash the empathy inside. Through striving to live out the "truths" of the New Testament, I have wounded friends and family. Any hurt I have caused in the wake of standing firm on what I was taught to believe is on me. It would be remiss for me not to mention the number of ways I have harmed many, many people in the name of Christianity. I was a victim of shame, yes, but I was dishing out the shame too.

I nearly broke up with a boyfriend for possessing a fake ID. That boyfriend was Beau.

I made fun of acquaintances who voted for Obama. Behind their backs, I called them "stupid" and "lost."

I confronted two friends on two separate occasions for dressing immodestly. I called up one out of the blue and blindsided her with my condemning assessment of her Instagram feed. I set up a dinner with the other, a dinner camouflaged as a "hang out."

I criticized a roommate who had sex before marriage. I'd felt sorry for her and her sinful ways.

I shook a finger at a family member who watched Game of Thrones. *The nudity.*

I looked down on my in-laws for drinking what I considered to be too much wine. (Two glasses.)

I prayed for people to change *who didn't need changing.* Worst of all, I silently judged my queer friends in my heart. It's the silent, judgmental concern that is the most toxic.

It devastates me to know that I am responsible for so much pain. It's hard to love and accept people when you don't love and accept yourself.

If you are a part of the LGBTQ+ community and have been hurt by the church, I am so sorry. Not being free to love and accept you for you was a me thing and not a you thing. For so long, I have been a part of organizations that have discriminated against queerness, and by association, I have too. I apologize for not owning my part and speaking up on your behalf. I wish I could repair all of the damage Christianity has done and is doing.

I am forever in awe of any human who is true to themselves. It takes serious guts to be your true self despite what anyone else thinks. Queer community, you have my utmost respect and admiration for choosing to be yourself in lieu of all the resistance. You trusted yourself through the flak of our society and followed your intuition. You being you gave me permission to be me. You being brave gave me the courage to be brave, too. Sometimes someone else has to do the hard thing before us so we can know that it's okay for us to do it, too.

You won't be surprised to know that I am fascinated by language. Language has the power to heal or hurt, help or fall short. I've referenced God a lot so far and I will continue to reference God. If the word "God" is triggering for you, I encourage you to swap it with another word or phrase that means something to you. It's not past me that the word "God" comes with a lot of baggage. Sometimes I call God "the Universe" or "the Divine". Language fails to describe that supernatural, transcendent and invisible force, higher power, presence, *energy*, that is lurking in all and through all. There's this thing behind the thing that is impossible to describe. And you have free rein to call it/he/she/they whatever you want.

I choose to believe God, the Universe, the Divine, loves us without a hidden agenda. I choose to believe that whoever or whatever the thing behind the thing is loves us without judgment. I choose to believe it/he/she/they love us freely. We are all humans. Humans, the ones with heartbeats, are not differentiated between dead or alive. There's alive, there's more alive, and there's even more alive, but none are dead. Supernatural joy has been hard-wired into our humanity. Supernatural peace is found within us. Both are there, waiting for us to tap in. All of us have access. All of us are one.

Polytheism

One of the first organized belief systems, Polytheism, was born around 3200 BCE. Early Polytheists believed in many gods, and the gods had dominion over the elements. Each god, assigned to either the sun, the moon, the stars, the clouds, etc., had full control over their area of expertise. Societies in that day and age did not have televised access to meteorologists, so they assumed it must be a god who was makin' it rain.

Another layer to Polytheism is that gods were anthropomorphic. Anthropomorphic means they were thought to have human qualities and temperaments. Since the gods mirrored the humans, the gods got frustrated from time to time. Polytheists believed if a natural disaster occurred, like an earthquake or flood, it was because they'd done something to upset the gods. If there was a drought for a long period of time, it was because the rain god was pissed. If you ask me, based on their limited knowledge, I think Polytheism is a fairly rational explanation of how sometimes it rained and sometimes it didn't.

Whether it was a pharaoh, king, emperor or chief, the leader of the people usually implemented structures that were highly influenced by Polytheistic beliefs. Strict rituals and traditions were set in place, and everyone in the community was expected to adhere. If you did not follow along, you were either punished or excommunicated from the clan. The only way to stay in the group and avoid getting chastised was to participate in the formalities without question.

Polytheists behaved in a way so as to placate the gods. Oftentimes, if a natural disaster occurred, like a drought, communities tried to make amends with the rain god. They'd make sacrifices and perform chants and dances and so on in attempts to reconcile. If it hadn't rained in a while and crops were dying, it was customary for the leader to want all hands on deck. And if the leader required a rain dance from the group, a rain dance it was. If an individual decided to sit out, the person could be shunned. Or worse, the belief was that the gods could potentially smite the person. The group as a whole did not want to pay the price (no rain) of one member's sin. Needless to say, the pressure was laid on thick for all individuals to perform.

Polytheists and Fundamentalists have a lot in common. Do you know how I was discouraged from looking into the Big Bang theory? I was curious about other theories on how the Earth was formed—besides the Garden of Eden. But, deep in Fundamentalist trenches, my mind gave me a hard stop. And remember how I felt ashamed after I kissed my churchy boyfriend on the cheek? I was behaving as if my action had upset the gods, similar to the Polytheists. I performed in a certain way to placate God. Plus, I was cut off from that romantic relationship because I did not adhere to complete and total "purity" guidelines.

I've been a part of eight Christian-inspired churches, two youth groups, two college ministries and one camp. The standards set in these organizations varied widely. Think not being allowed to pierce your nose, get tattoos or order an alcoholic beverage in public. Some requirements were so inflexible, such as men having to be clean-shaven, that Jesus himself would have gotten in trouble for his stylish beard. And *not one* of these organizations, ranging from mega Conservative to considerably Progressive, tolerated people who had sex before marriage or people in a gay relationship. It was intense. Being immersed in institutions such as those can feel like you're barefoot, and the ground you are forced to walk on is covered in eggshells.

Fundamentalist circles, and Christian circles in general, for example, have a devastatingly cruel tendency of penalizing a person for choosing to act in opposition to the traditions in the Bible. I cannot tell you how often I witnessed loved ones after loved ones being made to feel small when their vulnerabilities were exposed. Talk about petrifying. One bestie of mine was kicked off his church's leadership the second he came out as gay. Another close friend was stripped from the worship team because she announced she was living with her boyfriend. A loved one was fired from her job in ministry when her boss found out she was getting a divorce. Can you imagine?

I wish I could say I got off scot-free, yet I, too, have been publicly humiliated in the name of Christianity. As a camp counselor, I was scolded for shaking my butt too much in a line dance. Another time I wore a bikini to a beach get-together and was pulled aside by my small group leader. She told me I needed to put a t-shirt over my swimsuit top because I was responsible for making the other men lust. One time a pastor gave me a talking to for not tithing ten percent of my income to the church. And my personal favorite, I got "demoted" as a volunteer for questioning a pastor's decisions. All of these happened in my twenties. As dreadful as it is, the list goes on and on.

What's wild is that this type of behavior—behaving in a way to avoid upsetting the gods and shaming others who don't—dates back to 3200 BCE. It's like Polytheistic societies are rampant in the world today, just under the guise of different labels. It's as if those mindsets were passed down from generation to generation and us modern-day humans are still participating in those psychological thought processes. In 2021, there are people who interpret themselves, others and the world almost identically to how people interpreted themselves, others and the world in 3200 BCE. Say, what?

Chronic shame is a biggie side effect of rigid atmospheres. Being treated with such inferiority takes a toll on your heart. I can attest. What's sad is that because I was so close to this type of degradation, I thought it was normal. Worse, I thought it was *justified.* I thought it was justified to punish a person for not adhering to the rules of the Bible, church, camp, etc. I could not see beyond how I'd been conditioned. And, everyone I surrounded myself with had been conditioned in the same way. At the time, I did not have a tight-knit group of non-Christian friends who could offer an outside perspective. I stayed loyal to these organizations even though I was getting reprimanded repeatedly. What was I going to do, leave?

(YES!)

Eleanor Roosevelt said, "No one can make you feel inferior without your consent." I think this is half-true. Some environments lay the shame on thick, making it almost impossible not to feel disempowered. You cannot control what people say or do to you, but, in general, you can control who you surround yourself with. If you are in a community that makes you feel ashamed for just being you, you will most likely continue to feel ashamed. It is vital to either get out of that situation or set firm boundaries. Because, as you and I both know, that situation is unlikely to get better. And constantly being made to feel less than will continue to leave you in a disempowered state.

Groups heavily based on upholding religious or cultural constructs are uber difficult to move out of. First, it is likely that most of your relationships are with folks who are in the same group. I mean, imagine if your entire family and *all* of your friends were doing the rain dance. It'd be that much more difficult to stand your ground and sit it out. Second, there is a recognition that everyone in a given community believes in and upholds the same standards. So, if you dare to break a rule and have subsequently been labeled as "wrong," you might have to endure the punishments that pair with "rebelling." Like, being judged by the rest of your clique and potentially losing those friendships entirely.

There are a ton of healthy attributes of tight-knit, strict circles, too. For example, the recognition that two or more people joined together are stronger than an isolated individual, is huge. The family unit, the value of community, and the satisfaction of being a part of something bigger than yourself is lifegiving.

American philosopher Ken Wilbur introduced the phrase "transcend and include." To grow in a healthy manner, we must practice transcending and including. When distancing ourselves from toxic groups, it is essential to negate and break down the toxicity so that we can move beyond the boundaries that limit us and our thinking. But, while we surpass and *transcend* the limitations, you also *include* the valuable aspects. It's super important to take the good stuff with you. What you don't want to do is disregard and throw out all qualities because it will invite bitterness into your heart.

The most comprehensible way I can describe "transcend and include" is by providing some insight into Princess Elsa.

As one of the top-grossing animated films of all time, Disney's *Frozen* struck a chord with kids and adults alike. *Frozen* resonated with so many people when it was released in 2013 and still does to this day. Do you want to know why I think that is? Because Princess Elsa demonstrated a healthy transition out of a stifling situation.

At the beginning of the movie, Elsa discovers her icy powers. Afraid she might accidentally harm her sister, Ana, Elsa locks herself—and her power—in a bedroom. Elsa stays hidden in confinement to protect Ana. She sacrifices her own needs and limits her own capacity, for the sake of Ana's safety. Elsa's plan works for a while. Until it doesn't.

Understandably, Elsa begins to feel suffocated by the tight environment she put herself in. Elsa longs for an open space in which she can roam free and be her true self. She is haunted by the possibility that she is meant for more. Finally, Elsa realizes that she is holding herself back from unlocking her own potential by trying to protect Ana. Elsa runs away to a place that allows her to be vast, limitless. She breaks free of her chains and steps into self-empowerment.

Here's where the "transcend and include" part comes in. Once Elsa was able to be who she was meant to be, she found a way to reunite with her sister. She *transcended* by living out her truest self *and* she *included* her sister, Ana. Elsa and Ana coexisted, and not at the expense of Elsa's full potential. Transcend and include.

It is so important to strengthen our sense of selves and build our confidence. Reminder: your neural pathways are creatures of habit. If you dwell on how weak you are, the neural pathways for that belief become stronger. But if you dwell on how badass you are, the neural pathways for that belief become stronger. The pathways you create in your brain become your new normal, and you start to believe you are a badass. And if you believe you are a badass (you are!), then that belief has the potential to self-fulfill.

There are positive and negative attributes in most people circles, whether a religion, a start-up, or a Fortune 500. Being able to recognize the harmful *and* beneficial aspects of your community is a sign of growth. Once you posture your heart open to growth, the growth will come. It does not come without courage and sacrifice. But I promise you, it's worth it.

You are not a blind follower. You are not stuck. You are a freaking ice queen.

Flat Earth

We addressed how our beliefs, particularly smaller beliefs, can shift after we have been presented with incriminating evidence against them. But so often we are presented with incriminating data at odds with our existing beliefs, and we are *still* unlikely to switch our stance. Oftentimes we hang onto beliefs even *after* being confronted with blatant facts against them. Due to confirmation bias, we find our own data points to support our own conclusions.

Confirmation bias is the tendency to interpret evidence as a confirmation of one's existing beliefs or theories. In other words, if you are looking for "evidence" to support your belief in ____ or ____, you will find it. No matter what you believe, you will be able to back it up in some shape or form. Confirmation bias is dangerous because the "evidence" we find could be "fake news" for lack of a better term.

Core Beliefs re: False Evidence

A. Let's say I do not believe a potential partner is capable of loyalty. If my partner does not come home immediately after work, I will view that as evidence that they must be out cheating on me. Or, on the flip side, if my partner brings me flowers, I will view that gesture as proof they were unfaithful and are trying to make up for it.

B. Let's say I believe I am dumb. If I ever got a bad grade on a test, I'd see that bad grade as evidence that I am not smart. Or on the flip side, if I made a good grade on the test, I'd chalk that up to chance or luck and discount it.

A wonky fixed belief can be disastrous to our evolution of self because the "evidence" we run into might not be evidence at all. It might simply be our *perception* of evidence. Core beliefs are the lens through which we see things; therefore, the things we see are highly coated in what we already believe. In the hypothetical example of me believing I am dumb, I was internalizing a D or F grade as proof that I am dumb, when in fact, it's not proof at all. I just *think* it is because I am interpreting that D or F grade through the lens of believing I am dumb. In actuality, I am absolutely capable of intelligence, but I might not have studied enough for that test.

Beliefs are energy-saving shortcuts. Psychiatrist Ralph Lewis said,

> These shortcuts to interpreting and predicting our
> world often involve connecting dots and filling in gaps,

making extrapolations and assumptions based on incomplete information and based on similarity to previously recognized patterns. In jumping to conclusions, our brains have a preference for familiar conclusions over unfamiliar ones. Thus, our brains are prone to error, sometimes seeing patterns where there are none. It's a trade-off between efficiency and accuracy.

A faulty belief results in a faulty perception of reality. Since we interpret reality through the lens of our core beliefs, we must do our best to ensure the lens we see through is squeaky clean. Y'all, this is the hard stuff. Confirmation bias, similar to a fixed mindset, is a HUMP to get over. It's so much easier to remain stagnant by sticking to the same old evidence supporting what you already consider to be true. But what if the evidence you consider to be evidence is not actually evidence? What if it's merely your perception of evidence?

When Aristotle provided proof for a spherical Earth back in the 5th century BCE, not all people followed suit. Suddenly, humans were faced with a choice: believe Aristotle, adopt the new information, or hold on to the old. Because Aristotle's findings sharply contrasted long-standing beliefs, people were reluctant to adopt the new information. Civilizations in the

Bronze Age and Iron Age kept believing in a flat Earth for over 300 years after being presented with proof of a round Earth.

Even now, in postmodern America, there are flat-earthers, including rapper B.O.B. As of 2018, there are a reported 3,500 members of the Flat Earth Society of America (FESA). The group believes that scientists purposefully faked the data around a round Earth to lead people away from the biblical truth of a flat Earth.

Ashley Landrum, a psychologist from Texas Tech University, had the pleasure of attending the annual Flat Earth International Convention in 2018. Landrum reported that the event's curriculum included "14+ Ways the Bible Backs Up a Flat Earth" and how the flat-earthers need to start evangelizing by "sharing the truth about the earth's shape with their friends and families." Two of the 14 pieces of "evidence" used to reinforce a flat earth belief are in the Old Testament. "He has fixed the earth firm, immovable..." (Ps 96.10) and "Thou didst fix the earth on its foundation so that it never can be shaken" (Ps 104.5), both verses suggesting the earth does not rotate.

American physical anthropologist Eugenie Scott called members of the FESA an example of "extreme Biblical-literalist theology: the Earth is flat because the Bible says it is flat, regardless of what science tells us." It's not like modern-day flat-earthers have never seen the images of Earth from NASA. They have. But they've seen the proof and *rejected* it. After being presented with photographs of a spherical planet, flat-earthers conjured up their own version of evidence in the book of Psalm.

Diving into confirmation bias was a game-changer for me. The more I studied it, the more I understood why people like the flat-earthers are stuck in their beliefs. Although I did not fall into the flat-earther camp, I found evidence to support my own beliefs by using the exact same method as flat-earthers. I had a belief that God created the world in seven days, so I used the Bible as evidence to support that belief. I had a belief that sex before marriage was wrong, so I used the Bible as evidence to support that belief. I had a belief that homosexuality was wrong, so I translated the Bible to support that belief. Despite what science said or any experiences I'd had or heard about, my go-to reaction was to hang on to what the Bible said.

Do you recall how both right-wing Christians and left-wing Christians were drawing from the exact same text (the Bible), but gathering entirely different conclusions from it? The flat-earthers and me, a spherical-earther, are another example of this. Even in my homeschooling, I was taught that the Earth was round. The flat-earthers and I used the exact same text (the Bible) to back up what we already believed (aka confirmation bias). This happens because we read through the lens of our already crafted beliefs. Which group is interpreting this 2,000-year-old text correctly? Flat-earthers? Me? Both? Neither?

Do you see how dangerous it is to base your entire belief system on one specific text? Our brain connects the dots in a way that is so quick, we trade efficiency for accuracy. Whatever you *want* to believe, your brain is going to keep on finding supporting evidence for that belief, even if it's false proof. Many belief systems are based upon certain key texts seen as the One True Way. Science, data, facts, research, Democratic stance, Republican stance, the Constitution of the United States, the Bible, the Torah, the Koran, educational textbooks, the news, etc.

It's so important to consider *everything* when formulating our beliefs—emotions, thoughts, feelings, experiences, the state of the world, science, data, spirituality, and so on. All of it. If you only look at what a religious book says and ignore science, you won't know what to do when science debunks a facet of your religion. If you are only looking at science, you won't know what to do with a supernatural experience that science hasn't explained. Only landing on logical conclusions can be problematic too, because logic does not take empathy into consideration. It's vital to make sure we are taking every single aspect of life—everything we can think of—into consideration so that we are seeing a clear, whole picture.

The trouble with viewing one specific memo as the One True Way is two-fold: the memo could be out of date and the lens through which you interpret it could be erroneous.

When America's Founding Fathers established the Constitution in 1787, it took ten whole minutes to load a gun and fire it off. Our Founding Fathers added "a right to bear arms" to the document as a precaution. If the government revolted against the American people, they wanted Americans to be able to defend themselves. I appreciate that. Yet in 2021 our American government has over 5,800 nuclear warheads. Our government also has this thing called the Air Force. So even if every American person owned 15 AR15s, we still wouldn't stand a chance against our government. Not to mention the U.S. was wracked by a record-high 610 mass shootings in 2020. That averages out to nearly two mass shootings per day.

I'm going to go out on a limb and say that if our Founding Fathers were alive in 2021, they'd probably want to make adjustments to the Constitution. And that's exactly what amendments are for. We have amended the Constitution before and we can do it again. If we had left the Constitution as is, slavery would still be legal. Women would not be allowed to vote.

Black people would not be allowed to vote. Times have changed. It is crucial to update the document America was founded on in real-time.

If we are holding to tradition just for the sake of adhering to a certain document, there is a chance we are *abusing* the document. This occurs a lot with literature established hundreds of years ago or even thousands of years ago. The ancient literature in its original form was likely written to aid humanity. What aided humanity 300+ years ago most likely does not totally hold up in relevance nowadays. When much has evolved culturally, sticking to the way things have been done before can be problematic. Whoever designed the document way back then, like the Founding Fathers, might not agree with it in 2021 (God included).

When I first started dating Beau, we dated long-distance for two years. As someone whose love language is quality time, long-distance dating was rough. Our entire relationship was built on phone conversations and texts. To add to my woes, Beau was a dreadful texter. (He's since gotten much better.) I remember he sent me one text in particular that upset me.

Beau: How's your day?

Me: Hey, babe! Thanks for asking. Well, I went to class. It was alright. I got my nails done. I desperately needed a manicure.

And then I grabbed coffee with a friend. It's been a good day so far. Except now I'm about to head to the library to study for a test. Blah.

Beau: Cool.

Cool. Period?? My mind was reeling. I assumed I had blown it. I annoyed Beau with my lengthy text and he was over me. I thought he was for sure going to break up with me. Yet after a few days passed, nothing happened—no break-up call. I guess I was in the clear.

Much later in our relationship, I spoke with Beau about this scenario. He was shocked to hear my interpretation of his one-word text. He had no intention of me receiving the message how I did. In actuality, the dude just sucked at texting. He genuinely thought my day sounded "cool." That is a one-word text taken out of context and interpreted erroneously. Imagine all of the ways we misinterpret a whole book or document! The bottom line is that humans are imperfectly perfect. We make mistakes. Even in how we interpret religious books, data, facts, science, etc.

Most texts that have stood the test of time have done so for a reason. The trueness of these texts still resonates with its readers in 2021, no matter when it was transcribed, which is amazing and intriguing and kind of a miracle. There are beautiful, creative works of art that some of the most popular religions in the world are founded upon, and abiding by its guidelines has proven advantageous. But in the end, those works are collections of wise and powerful sentences and not *all* we can look at. To quote *Pirates of the Caribbean*'s Captain Barbossa: "The code is more what you call guidelines than actual rules."

Believing we have the right map, correct answers or secret sauce to what it means to be human, in my opinion, is devolved thinking—especially with Confirmation Bias at play. Because even if we have evidence to back up our truths, how can we know for sure that the evidence we have is legit?

I think the world would be a better place if we all relinquished the idea that our beliefs are founded upon the One True Way. If we can start to not view life as black and white, but as grey and nuanced, we will open ourselves up to evolving. Being attached to wrongs and rights keeps us chained to sameness.

A move out of a black and white thinking style sounds simple and easy, but it's pretty darn scary and complicated. It's a move out of the known and into the unknown. It's a move out of the comfortable and into the uncomfortable. It's knowing that you don't know. Black and whites provides a false sense of control, whereas greys give up control. But, to me, letting go is worlds more enjoyable than operating under the illusion that we are in control. Because detaching from absolutes and certainties is freeing.

Coke

Recently I watched a film titled *The Gods Must Be Crazy*, a comedy from 1980 directed by Jamie Uys. The movie opens with a scene of a man flying over the Kalahari Desert in Southern Africa. The guy is in a four-seater Cessna jet, and he is soaking up the nice weather with the windows rolled down. The man sips from a glass bottle of Coke. He takes his last gulp and tosses the Coca-Cola out the window of the airplane. Classic.

The glass bottle lands, fully intact, in the center of a remote village. The villagers who live in the desert, called the San tribe, are totally off-the-grid. The San tribe works with materials like wood and bone; this is their first encounter with glass. Plus, they have not met other people besides their own, nor have they seen an airplane close enough to identify it. Needless to say, the San tribe members are puzzled as to how the bottle of Coke got to them.

Xi, one of the tribe members, stumbles upon the bottle. He and the other members deliberate on how the bottle got there and what it even is. From their perspective, the bottle appears to have fallen from the heavens. Eventually, the villagers concluded that the glass bottle of Coca-Cola must be a gift to them from the gods above. Xi sets out to return the gift; he wants to extend his thanks to the gods personally. He exits the comfort of his tribe and journeys to experience a whole new realm: civilization.

From the outside looking in, it's obvious that the glass bottle is not a gift from the gods. But to Xi and his tribe, given their limited view of the world, a gift from the gods was a plausible explanation as to how it got there. How could they know it fell from an airplane when they don't know what an airplane is?

The world around us is like a bubble. Some bubbles are more diverse than others, but they are bubbles nonetheless. The folks surrounding us are likely to align with our viewpoints. Sometimes we surround ourselves with people who align with our viewpoints on purpose, and sometimes it's something that happens naturally due to our geographical location. It's important to note that the news we receive via FOX, CNN or social media, is geared to tell us what we want to hear. Sometimes we turn on the news station that tells us what we want to hear on purpose, and other times it's unintentional. To pop our environmental bubbles, we must intentionally switch up our environments.

Switching up your environment does not have to be physical. If packing up and moving is not in the cards for you, have no fear. Diversifying your atmosphere is as simple as purposefully switching the news station or listening to a podcast you once deemed off-limits. It's as minute as watching a documentary about opposing religions, doctrines and politics. It's challenging the status quo and investigating.

A while back, I watched a segment on police brutality by Tucker Carlson. Carlson was questioning the legitimacy of police officers' racial profiling. His argument included a statistic on how many white people were killed by the police per year versus how many Black people were killed by the police per year. The statistic he shared was 60/40, as in 60 percent *white* and 40 percent Black.

I was living in my bubble (Los Angeles) at the time I watched this segment. To be honest, I was pretty surprised by that statistic. I would have thought it would be flipped, and it didn't seem right. So I looked into it. I spoke with knowledgeable friends, scoured the Interwebs and listened to podcasts on police brutality. Digging up a bit of research, I found the facts Tucker Carlson shared were indeed correct. Interesting.

What I also found is the ratio of white people to Black people in America. According to the 2019 U.S. Census Bureau, Black people make up only 13.4 percent of the population. The fact that the percentage of Black people killed by the police per year is that close to the percentage of white people killed by the police per year is appalling. Carlson failed to mention the full scope of the situation.

By listening to Tucker Carlson, I got one piece of the puzzle. By listening to CNN, I got another piece of the puzzle. By researching statistics, I got another piece of the puzzle. By talking to a Black friend, I got another piece of the puzzle. By talking to another Black friend, I got another piece of the puzzle. By talking to my white friend whose dad is a police officer, I got another piece of the puzzle. Finally, by talking to my Black friend whose husband is a police officer, I got another piece of the puzzle.

To be honest I am hesitant to share this example. I am not out to get Tucker Carlson. There is so much polarization in today's world, and I am not looking to add to the mix. When we split the country into two separate sides, it creates division. I am not asking you to see the "other" side. There are not many issues that are only two-sided. Life is nuanced and complicated. I am encouraging you to see *all* sides.

Like Xi's character in *The Gods Must Be Crazy*, we often hold a wonky belief because we flat out don't know any better. Yet you and I do not have the same excuse as Xi. In our modern-day, we have access to unlimited knowledge with the tap of a screen. It takes a little intentionality and time to seek out knowledge, but it's worth it when there's a chance we could find a missing piece to the puzzle. If we are only gathering information from inside our bubbles, our entire belief system could be based on either false or skewed information.

Knowledge is like a chiliagon, a polygon with 1,000 sides. If we're lucky, our bubbles might show us ten sides of that chiliagon. I don't know about you, but I do not want to form a belief from a limited perspective. We must keep turning the chiliagon and check out at all its sides to gain understanding.

Coal

I was just shy of six years old the Christmas my dad got coal in his stocking. On Christmas Eve, I did all the things. I chopped up carrots and sprinkled them in the front yard for the reindeer. Mom and I decorated sugar cookies and filled up a glass of milk for Santa. After I set the cookies and milk on the fireplace, I tucked myself into bed.

The next morning, I woke up at an ungodly hour, jumped on my parents, and dragged them into the living room. I pulled down the stockings from the mantle on the fireplace. That's when I saw it. Santa gave Dad coal in his stocking. As a six-year-old, I thought it was the funniest thing ever, and as a 27-year-old, I still do. It made me so devilishly giddy to think that Santa Claus put my pops on his naughty list.

A few months later, I lost my first tooth. I placed the tooth under my pillow for the tooth fairy to collect. The following morning, I awoke to no tooth and 25 cents. I brought the quarter to school and bragged to my fellow kindergarteners. That's when

I found out the tooth fairy needed a lesson on equality. One girl in my class said she got five dollars. What the frick?

A know-it-all kid blurted, "The tooth fairy is your parents!" As soon as he spoke those words, I knew he was right. I felt the truth sink into the depths of my soul, and kindergarten me started to connect the dots. If the tooth fairy is my parents, what about Santa Claus? If Santa's not real, who put coal in my dad's stocking? *My dad?*

I got home and asked my mom to tell me the truth, point-blank. After a couple of dodges, she confirmed my suspicions: the whole thing was all a scam. In a matter of hours, a fantastical universe I once wholeheartedly believed in had evaporated. Rudolph, Donner, Cupid, Blitzen, Mrs. Claus, the North Pole, the elves, the Tooth Fairy, Santa, vanished. Gone. I buried my head in my mom's lap and burst into tears. I was heartbroken.

I think it's time for a refresher.

- You and I are made up of core beliefs and thousands of smaller beliefs.

- Our core beliefs were formed in childhood.

- Our smaller beliefs were formed through the lens of our core beliefs.

- Our smaller beliefs can be affected when presented with incriminating evidence (*real* evidence) against them.

- Or, our smaller beliefs can be affected when we have a contradictory experience.

- Our core and smaller beliefs are connected.

- If a smaller belief is affected, it can start a domino effect.

- If a smaller belief is affected, it can ultimately take down a core belief.

- If a core belief is affected, it can ultimately take down the system as a whole.

I love a good bulleted list.

I had zero doubts about Santa before I heard an opinion in opposition to my belief in the Tooth Fairy. I was pretty positive Santa existed, considering the coal and everything. But once my baby belief in the Tooth Fairy collapsed, it eventually led to my big mama belief in Santa collapsing too. When my big mama belief in Santa collapsed, the system in totality fell to the ground. And it royally sucked.

It's not fun having your belief system unravel. When I found out Santa wasn't real, I was frustrated at my parents for lying to me. And I was frustrated at myself for believing the lie. It hurt. All of that heartbreak over Santa Claus. Can you imagine how brutal it'd be if your adult belief system suddenly evaporated?

If you are exposed to radically different thoughts and beliefs that put your current belief system into question, you are likely to experience emotions such as anxiety, anger, confusion, shock or frustration. It can be a painful process. Consider yourself warned about the unraveling of your belief system. I don't want you to be blindsided. I do want you to be prepared. I am anchoring your expectations: it gets messier before it gets tidier.

Human brains are complex. Your brain is fully aware that a modification in a tiny belief is like a crack in a foundation. Your brain knows that sooner or later, the house could come down. And if the house comes down, it's going to hurt. That's why the frontal lobe works overtime via homeostasis to make sure you do not change *any* of your current beliefs—smaller or core.

If there's confusion or chaos or mystery, homeostasis strives to maintain order by sticking with what we know. The frontal lobe is the part of the brain that is structured around a natural resistance to change. Homeostasis demands a physiological state of stability. Obviously, our brains are capable of learning and adapting, but these adaptations are ultimately in the service of maintaining homeostasis. Homeostasis runs the show and is driven by the fear of getting hurt.

This would explain yet another reason why we experience confusion when unlearning our beliefs. It is easier to resolve this discomfort by doubling down on our existing belief system—ignoring or explaining away the challenging, contradictory information. On one hand, it's nice of our brains to try and protect us from the humiliation and suffering that comes with the disruption of a belief system. On the other hand, it's a contributing factor to the crisis of personal and cultural stagnancy and self-made cages.

Our belief systems can come crashing down in a matter of minutes, kind of like a mudslide. With a mudslide, a large mass of wet earth suddenly and quickly moves down the side of a mountain or hill, and it's strong enough to take down a house. It can come out of nowhere.

It's more common for our belief systems to fall apart over very lengthy periods of time, like a foundational creep. A foundational creep is the gradual downward movement of disintegrated rock or soil due to gravitational forces. It's the sum of numerous minuscule, discrete movements of slope material. The gravitational force perpendicular to the slope decreases and results in less friction between the material that could cause the slope to slide. Eventually, the ground can shift the foundation.

Gypsy Rose Blanchard, born in 1991, was raised by her single mom in semi-isolation. Her mother, Dee Dee Blanchard, taught Gypsy to believe that she had leukemia and muscular dystrophy. Among other health issues, according to Dee Dee, Gyspy had been diagnosed with sleep apnea, seizures, epilepsy, asthma and a life-threatening allergy to sugar.

In actuality, Gyspy was quite healthy, and it turns out Dee Dee was the unwell one. Dee Dee had a mental disorder called Munchausen syndrome by proxy, which presents as a caretaker exaggerating or feigning sickness in another person to get attention and sympathy for themselves. In her own illness, Dee Dee went to extreme measures in faking her daughter's.

Since children who actually have cancer typically experience hair loss from chemotherapy, Dee Dee routinely shaved Gypsy's head. Since people living with muscular dystrophy usually require assistance walking, Gypsy traveled to and fro via wheelchair. She slept with a breathing machine and consumed all of her meals by a feeding tube per her mother's insistence. Up until her late teens, Gypsy's life was structured around fabrications.

Eating a cupcake triggered Gypsy Rose Blanchard's belief system to self-destruct. The appropriately named Hulu true-crime series, *The Act*, is modeled after both Blanchard women. Gypsy, played by Joey King, puts her existing beliefs to the test during a neighbor's birthday party in the TV show. Knowing full well that she is supposedly deathly allergic to sugar, Gypsy snags a cupcake when Dee Dee, played by Patricia Arquette, is not looking.

Gypsy bravely risks her life to find out the truth: does she or does she not have a sugar allergy?

Of course, Gypsy's body does not react to the cupcake whatsoever, apart from enjoying the taste. Nevertheless, Dee Dee still rushes her to the emergency room. After the cupcake fiasco, the drama depicts Gyspy gradually connecting the dots. If her mom lied to her about the sugar allergy, what else could she have lied about?

In the show, once Gypsy unlearns her belief about sugar, she opens herself up to the idea that she does not have leukemia, muscular dystrophy or any of the other falsely diagnosed diseases. Gradually over time, her core beliefs about herself—including that she is terminally ill—are affected after the smaller belief about sugar is affected. In the end, Gypsy's entire world comes undone. It unravels.

Whether it happens suddenly or over a spread-out period of time, I believe the unlearning process is a lot like the grief process. Swiss-American psychiatrist Elizabeth Kübler-Ross concluded in her book, *On Death and Dying*, that grief can be divided into five stages: denial, anger, bargaining, depression, acceptance. If our belief system collapses, we are likely to experience all of these stages of grief. We grieve our old beliefs.

I know it sounds dramatic, but I had to let Santa die before I could move on to the next chapter of my life. I had to accept that he was gone. It hurt little-kid me to say goodbye to Santa. I had to be angry and sad for a while. I had to be angry and sad before I could make peace with the fact that Christmas would never be the same. Believing in Rudolph and the North Pole was so magical for me. Even so, I am grateful that the fantastical world of mystical characters was shattered. If anything, it would be a tad odd if I still believed in Santa. Santa dying allowed me to reconstruct my perception of reality more accurately.

The more intense the brainwashing, the more painful the process of deconstructing will be. As I'm sure you can imagine, Gypsy was furious with her mom—she was legitimately brainwashed. We have to grieve what we were taught, even when it's clearly for the best to move on. If you ever find yourself in this situation, allow yourself to experience all of the grief stages. Let the phases do their work in your internal world. Take the time you need to heal. Oh, and have empathy for yourself. For goodness sake, you were borderline brainwashed! How could you not believe what you were taught?

To get to transformation, you must go through the mourning of the old. I feel like I'm trying to prepare someone for labor pains. It can help to know that the contractions are coming and to brace yourself, but unfortunately, they're still going to be painful. When life is heavy, sit in the heaviness. Take it in and reflect; don't ignore it. Wait for hope to appear because it will. I promise you, hope will come. The light will emerge. It always does. When there's a death, there's a birth. When there's an end, there's a beginning.

Palm Springs

A few summers ago, I took a road trip to Palm Springs. The company I worked for at the time put on a two-night and three-day all-staff retreat. We were there for one goal and one goal only: team building. Most of the programming took place in a mansion similar to the one in Brian De Palma's film *Scarface*. Over-the-top, old and a little creepy with malfunctioning AC. Outside, the temperature was an ungodly 115 degrees. Needless to say, we were a sweaty group.

There was a guest speaker; we'll call him Tom. Tom, also sweaty, coached my colleagues and me on the ins and outs of effective communication. He talked us through what constructive candor looks like and what it doesn't look like. He said a bit about feedback and a bit about gossip. I must say, despite the heat, this Tom guy had our attention.

Then Tom said it was time for breakouts. Breakouts? He proceeded to divide our whole group of 60 into miniature pods of five. He gave us a prompt. Each pod member was instructed to take turns answering this question: *When was the last time you changed your mind?*

Easy enough. A woman in my pod volunteered to kick us off. We'll call her Mary. We told her to go for it. Mary said that for most of her life, exercise and healthy eating did not appeal her. She quite enjoyed a lifestyle free of spinach and sit-ups. Until one day.

Mary paid a visit to her primary doctor. What began as a routine check-up turned into an intervention. Mary's doctor expressed concern for her well-being. *Mary, your current diet and lifestyle could be jeopardizing your health.*

Mary said she felt overwhelmed after that appointment. She'd hit a hurdle with no choice but to jump over.

Mary started walking. She walked to the post office, to the mall, to her friends' houses. As it turns out, she loves to walk. Then, Mary switched up her diet. She made grilled chicken instead of fried. She put spinach in her smoothies. She discovered almond milk. To her surprise, she loved exercising her body and feeding it nutrients.

Mary proudly announced to us that she'd lost over 50 pounds. She said she found herself where she least expected: in changing. Because she changed her mind, she saved her life.

What transpired—and perspired—in an overheated mansion in Palm Springs caught me off guard. I listened as my coworkers, one by one, shared glimpses into their before and afters. From unhealthy to well, corporate to art, dating men to dating women. A sense of hope hung in the air. We were present. Who knew changing our minds was this dynamic?

Each of our stories shared a common theme: a death, then a birth. An ending is actually a beginning. *The old has gone; the new has come.*[vi] To get to the new, a disruption of the present must occur. With each disruption, we are faced with a choice: old or new? Past or future? Preservation or expansion?

Sameness is fine. It's completely, totally, utterly fine. There's nothing wrong with sameness. Newness is the juice of life. It's risky, yes. And it is invigorating and challenging and adventurous. What'll it be? Fine? Or invigorating and challenging and adventurous?

Mars

The classroom was space-themed. While the adults listened to an old white dude preach about boring stuff, we third graders got to board a rocket ship. Every Sunday, along with 20 other eight-year-olds, I pretended to be an astronaut. We sat down on a large, star-shaped rug and did our best impression of floating in zero-gravity. The lessons began when our fearless leader, who had a celestial name, like Arpina or Xenon, appeared as a 2-D projection on the back wall of the "spacecraft." It was the early 2000s, after all.

Arpina/Xenon: Hello, space cadets! Who's ready to explore the galaxy?

Us: Meeeeeeeeeeeeee!

Arpina/Xenon: You know the magic words!

Us: BLAST OFF!

The lead cadet's image was replaced with a "live" feed of the universe. Our spaceship skyrocketed through the dark sky, passing asteroids on our left and shooting stars on our right. Up ahead we saw a couple of moons and a giant red planet.

We were transported to Mars, where Satan lived.

Arpina/Xenon's voice was heard loudly over the speakers: Astronauts! We could be in grave danger. Stay alert.

Ten seconds later, Satan popped up on the screen. He looked like a big blob of fire, his face made up of red flames, and his hair and eyelashes consisting of blue flames. His piercing eyes were snake-like. Satan was terrifying.

Satan: Muhahahahaha! You thought you could get past me? Think again!

Arpina/Xenon's voice came through calm but urgent: Space cadets, we need your help. You must defeat Satan! Do you remember how to crush him?

Us: Yessssss!

Arpina/Xenon: On the count of three. One, two... three!

Us: JESUS IS LORD! JESUS IS LORD! JESUS IS LORD!

Satan spiraled into a black hole.

Laughter! Cheering!

In that extra-terrestrial Sunday School class, I learned where you go after you die if you did *not* invite Jesus to live in your heart. You go to hell.

Hell is the opposite of heaven. Hell is everlasting death. It's not *really* on Mars, but it is where Satan lives, and it is an eternal fiery furnace. Everyone who does not say The Prayer is tortured in hell after their death, forever scorched. Therefore, it was of utmost importance to share the gospel to ensure others did not spend eternity in flames.

All of us eight-year-olds were shown a series of video clips convincing us to tell others about Jesus. One animated short is impossible to forget. In it, a man walks past a fountain. He notices an infant in the water of the fountain, about to drown. The man hesitates. He stares at the baby. Tragically, he decides to keep walking. He lets the baby die. We were told if we do not tell others about Jesus, we too would be like that man—leaving the rest of the world to drown in a fountain.

Another clip, not animated, was set in a big city. A woman is shown crossing a busy street. Out of nowhere, a semi-truck runs a red light and speeds towards her. A bystander quickly takes in his surroundings and intervenes. In the nick of time, he jumps out into the oncoming traffic and tackles the woman into safety. The truck zooms by. The bystander saves the woman's life.

Proselytizing was serious business. It was life or death, and we were saving lives.

The lessons made me feel wretched. I did not want anyone to go to hell. I took it upon myself to tell anyone I could think of about Jesus. I oriented elementary, middle school, high school, college and my early 20s around trying to save the world from an afterlife of despair. I approached playmates, neighbors, Uber drivers, waitresses and flight attendants. If talking about Jesus could save a soul, even just one, I was willing to do it. I wanted to do everything in my power to make sure no human would have to meet Satan.

Not all of my Christian friends had the same approach. I had trouble coming to terms with their lack of urgency. If we could save a person's soul by proselytizing, then shouldn't we be going door to door? Shouldn't we be holding up a sign on a street corner and shouting with a megaphone? I had no interest in committing social suicide, but I thought that a matter of everlasting life or death was worth sacrificing my pride. I looked around at the Christians in my life and thought, why are we not living a bit more *radically*?

I had heard about missionaries who dedicated their existence to preaching the Good News, which seemed like a rational response! Apart from them, I felt like I was carrying this dismal burden alone. Fed up, I unloaded my internal monologue onto one of my mentors in college. She pointed me to a verse in Matthew that read, "Small is the gate and narrow the road that leads to life, and only a few find it." I was told the scripture meant only a teeny tiny percentage of humans were going to heaven. It blew my mind that God included *me* in that teeny tiny percentage. How did I get so lucky? My mentor tried to assure me that it wasn't my responsibility to rescue non-believers. People had to find the narrow road (Jesus) on their own terms. I could remove the weight from my shoulders.

I left that conversation feeling even more hopeless. It left me feeling *helpless*. On one hand, I was relieved not to have to convert the majority of the world's population. On the other hand, the majority of the world's population was doomed, and there was nothing I could do about it. I was enormously thankful I had been exposed to The Truth. But it was hard for me to enjoy my salvation knowing the bleak fate that awaited a massive portion of humanity. The thought of God allowing that many humans to be handed over to Satan was a tough pill for me to swallow. How would I be able to enjoy my time in heaven if meanwhile, my Catholic grandparents and Agnostic cousins were getting tortured?

I had some questions.

Later on, I heard about a man named Rob Bell. I don't remember who I was with or what I was doing the first time I heard about Rob Bell. I do, however, remember what was said about him. One of Bell's books stirred up quite a controversy in my Christian circles. He released a book titled *Love Wins: A Book About Heaven, Hell, and the Fate of Every Person Who Ever Lived.* (The title is a joke because how could a human authoritatively write in detail on a subject that has not yet been revealed to us earthlings? I wasn't in on the joke.)

Person: Have you heard of Rob Bell?

Me: No.

Person: Rob Bell is a Christian who doesn't believe in hell.

Me: A Christian who doesn't believe in hell? Is it even possible to be a Christian who doesn't believe in hell?

I had some questions.

So, I did what any rational human would do: I placed my questions in a cardboard box, duct-taped it shut and stored it in the attic of my soul. For years, this is where my box of questions sat and collected dust. I found it was much easier to suppress my curiosity than to face it. And it was much easier to stand firm on the foundation of what I was taught than to confront my suspicions.

It wasn't that I had never heard other ideas regarding the afterlife. I had. But when I was presented with reincarnation, samsara, and purgatory theories, I interpreted them through the lens of heaven and hell being the right theory. Moreover, I learned about the religions of the world in a course called Apologetics. Apologetics is a class designed to inform you about other religions in the event that you need to *defend* Christianity. Not once did I open my heart to consider any other beliefs regarding the afterlife, only my own.

Until 2020.

In an effort to stay awake, I force myself to take another swig of the shitty Lipton tea pooled in a Styrofoam cup. A Human Resources conference is just about as fun as it sounds. Twenty of us HR professionals rocking name tags and doing our best to absorb an ungodly amount of legal information in the basement of a Holiday Inn in San Diego, California. Easily the youngest person in the room by at least ten years, I checked the time on my iPhone for the tenth time in the past ten minutes. The instructor, who reminded me of Mrs. Doubtfire, was finally wrapping up her second two-hour lecture of the day. Thankfully so, because my stomach was growling for some lunch.

One of my favorite elements of California is its actual elements. The weather's average daily high temperature hovers around 70°F and up, permitting outdoor eating at almost any moment in a given year. I chose to spend my one-hour break reading and munching outside on the patio of a Starbucks near the hotel. Unwrapping half of my spinach-and-feta wrap for it to cool, I snagged my Bible from my tote and cracked it open on the table. I read,

> Women should remain silent in the churches. They are not allowed to speak but must be in submission, as the law says. If they want to inquire about something, they should ask their own husbands at home, for it is disgraceful for a woman to speak in the church. (1 Cor 14.34-35 NIV)

This verse gave me pause. Although still too hot to eat, I took a bite of my food and pondered: if I am looking for spiritual guidance, I should go home and ask my husband? What does he know? (Love you, Babe.) This is not Leviticus or Deuteronomy, Old Testaments books, this is 1 Corinthians we're talking about. New Testament ish, written by Paul post-Jesus. Jesus doesn't seem like the type to oppress women... would Jesus agree with Paul's words?

In Fundamentalism, the Bible is to be interpreted literally and lived out accordingly—*especially* the verses in the New Testament.

With that in mind, I was baffled by the way Paul addresses women in his letter to the Corinthians. The implications of being obedient to Paul's words would mean silencing myself in public. Silencing myself in *church*. Does God want me to be silenced? Does God want me to submit to any ol' male pastor? Or to my husband? Or both?

Long after the HR convention ended, this passage in the Bible continued to bug me. I decided to ask around. I interrogated pastors, theologians, and small group leaders and hit them with my questions. I received similar responses from each person. I was told over and over that women remaining quiet in the church was a cultural thing way back then. My spiritual authority figures guaranteed it was a-okay for me to speak up nowadays. A woman's voice is not a sin. *Whew.*

I had a follow-up question. What about this verse, also written by Paul?

> God gave them over to shameful lusts. Even their women exchanged natural sexual relations for unnatural ones. In the same way, the men also abandoned natural relations with women and were inflamed with lust for one another. Men committed shameful acts with other men and received in themselves the due penalty for their error. (Rom 1.26-27 NIV)

I asked *it's cool for people to be gay then, right?* All of the people I asked, every single one, without hesitation, in all confidence, said, "No."

No? But how do you know?

Let me get this straight: over 2,000 years ago, Paul wrote two letters, one to a church in Corinth and one to a church in Rome. We don't have to listen to what he says in one letter anymore due to the cultural progression. But what he says in the other letter, we do have to listen to despite the cultural progression? Who gets to decide which verses we listen to and which ones we don't? A lot can change in 2,000 years. Heck, a lot can change in two months. If Paul were alive today, would he stand by his words? What would Jesus think of Paul's words?

It's tough to imagine Jesus labeling a loving, gay relationship as shameful. It's tough to imagine Jesus endorsing any sort of discrimination based on race, gender or sexual orientation. I'd been a part of eight churches at this point. Four in Arkansas, one in Texas and two in Los Angeles. All of those churches did not support gay marriage or an openly gay pastor. So much so, they took the time to write their objections to homosexuality in their bylaws. I grew increasingly skeptical. A gay relationship was considered to be a sin. You know what else is considered to be a sin? Gluttony. How come "Pastors shall not eat too much cake" is not written in the bylaws? Gee, probably because that would be *cruel.*

You know what else is considered to be a sin? Gossip. Pride. Racism. I couldn't help but wonder, if it's all sin, who chose which ones to highlight and which ones to ignore? I tried to wrap my brain around the concept of respectable sins in the Christian community. Gluttony, gossip, pride, racism, all totally understandable. Homosexuality? Err! Wrong answer. Is anyone else confused by this? Okay, hear me out, new plan... instead of churches not hiring gay leaders, how about churches not hiring racist leaders?

More and more I started to see a double standard. More and more, to me, it looked like Christians cherry-picked the Bible.

Something felt off. Something felt fishy. Something was up.

Who is making the rules here?

2020: the year the world paused. Crisis hit. Distractions faded into the abyss. The hustle and bustle slowed to a stop. I was left alone with my questions. Disaster first, healing second.

I sliced through the tape of my questions box. It was as if I'd unpacked a Casper mattress. At first, I desperately tried to stuff it back in. You know how impossible that is if you've ever ordered a Casper mattress. The questions led to more questions, which led to more questions. At one point, there was no turning back; it was too late. The only option was for me to see the queries through and follow where they led. Like a knitted sweater, I pulled apart my beliefs thread by thread until I was left with a pile of tangles. It was messy yet electrifying.

Before immersing myself in the murky, angsty, spiritually enchanted waters of wrestling with doubt, *knowing* had been my religion. Operating from a place of knowing all there is to know prevented me from going there, from addressing the fears whirling in my soul. Somehow my inner world managed to suffocate the intriguing, mysterious, magic of life as a human into a checklist of certainties. Blacks and whites. Wrongs and rights. Yeses and nos.

The problem with a black and white list is this: life is nuanced. *God is grey.* He's depth, not yeses and nos. Compressing God into a manifest of *this and not that* is like condensing the world wide web into a single tweet. The draw of God is *the mystery.* God is mystifying, transcendent, a loss for words, intriguing, thrilling. Yet, I had thought I had Him pegged.

In the Bible, God describes himself to Moses as "I Am who I Am." As in, no need to peg him down. To reduce I Am down to a substance that I can remotely wrap my head around—like truths and untruths—is, to put it delicately, a disservice. I was exchanging this provocative, unexplainable Being for a set of rules in a text. Abiding by the literal interpretation of the Bible was like a pair of crutches. A pair of crutches that lent themselves useful for a season, but kept me from walking on my own. What once aided me now hurt me. Falling back on the Scriptures became a comfort zone that hindered my growth.

Harvard psychology professor Ellen J. Langer said, "Certainty is a cruel mindset. It hardens our minds against possibility." As a Christian, I was certain I had the answers in the Bible. I did not allow my heart to ask certain questions. I could ask stuff like, "Is sex before marriage wrong?" but I would not dare question the cornerstones of my faith. How backward is that? Isn't it that much more important to look into the cornerstones—the erroneous Word of God, heaven, hell, Jesus' resurrection, The Trinity, sin—of the faith I'm building my life upon? I was doubling down on a religion I knew very little about. I did not know that in 325 CE, the Council of Nicaea decided Jesus was equal to God and banished the Arian leaders who disagreed for "heresy." I did not know Martin Luther argued for the book of James not to be included in the Bible, calling it "an epistle of straw." Serious question: when Jesus mentions hell in the gospels, is it possible Jesus was referring to a *figurative* hell?

All of us have guesses as to what awaits us in the afterlife. We have theories, scientific and religious. I get why my Christian friends did not want to proselytize. It feels weird trying to persuade another human to adopt your guess. It doesn't quite sit right. My guess is it's something good. The universe is rigged for our growth.[vii] When something bad happens, any bad thing, something good can come from it. The universe is designed to produce beauty from ashes. Even in the darkest of the dark moments in life, I can look back on and see the good. When there is a death, there is a rebirth. A death and then a death no longer holds up for me. When the old has gone, the new will come. Newness is good. I am choosing to believe that when humanity is turned to ash, there will be beauty.

I think I understand what Jesus was talking about when he said, "The truth shall set you free."

The truth is, I don't have the answers. Can you feel the freedom in that? I found freedom in letting go of the concept of hell. I found freedom in no longer living in fear of hell. There is so much freedom to be found in *not* pretending to know the mind or nature of God. I don't know the mind or nature of God, but I am choosing to believe that whatever or whoever God is is *for* humanity, inclusive and loving to all.

I used to believe women in leadership positions were wrong. I used to believe sex before marriage was wrong. I used to believe queerness was wrong. I used to believe I knew what came after death. I used to believe a lot of things until I encountered incriminating evidence against those beliefs. When my smaller beliefs were affected, over time, it affected my core beliefs like a domino effect. When my core beliefs were affected, they unraveled the whole system. I took my faith *so* seriously, so much so that I looked into it. And because I looked into it, it crumbled.

Jesus said, "Seek and you shall find." What if seeking *is* finding? Is it possible that those who seek truth are not lost but rather found because they seek it? What if truth is not set in stone, but liquid and fluid? Who we are and what we are doing here is a mystery. American author Richard Rohr said, "Mystery isn't something that you cannot understand—it is something that you can endlessly understand!"[viii] It's like an asymptote, a line that continually approaches a given curve but does not meet it at any finite distance. Understanding is the y-axis and searching are the x-coordinates, which tend to infinity. There's eternally more to discover, and it's intoxicating. It's an adrenaline rush.

Is there a God?

Is there a heaven?

Is there a hell?

Who are we?

What are we doing here?

What is this?

Who am I?

What if spirituality is less about answers and more about questions? I wonder what would happen if instead of holding on to our beliefs for dear life, we let go?

Interlude: Parents

Mom,

I thought you had to say I was talented because you are my mom. I realize now, you didn't have to, yet you did. Thank you. Thank you for raising me to pursue my dreams.

You are a homemaker in the kindest sense. You showed me what it looks like to kick my shoes off and stay awhile. You taught me how to belly-laugh. You embody warmth. I'm taking notes.

I love you as you are,

Sarah

Dad,

I see how you fight for me. I see how you fight for all of your kids; you put us first. I am proud to call you my dad.

Thank you for teaching me to be generous with my time and money. Thank you for teaching me how to ask for help.

You are a beacon of hope. If a complete stranger is having a bad day, just your presence makes it brighter.

I admire you,

Sarah

The Abyss

Deconstructing my beliefs evoked something unexpected: death. When you build your world around a faith and have doubts about that faith, it can be traumatizing.

It's like the stock market; the more you have invested, the more painful a crash can be. I attached my identity, friends, behaviors, politics, interests, clothes, music, mind, body and heart to a religion. I did not half-ass Christianity. I was all in. And if you're all in, a crash is devastating. The old me died.

But when there is a death, there is a rebirth.

Progressive Christian to human.

Sarah Blake to Sarah the Human.

I grieved the old. I experienced anxiety, anger, confusion, shock, frustration. I feared the new.

In Joseph Campbell's *Hero's Journey*, all heroes enter an abyss. The *Hero's Journey* is often used as a template for heroes written in the scripts of movies and books. A hero first hears a call to adventure. The hero then has to cross the threshold of Known to Unknown. When challenges arise, the hero is tempted to return to the Known. In the midst of temptation, there is confusion and fear. Amidst the confusion and fear, the hero enters the abyss. In the abyss, a hero experiences a death and a rebirth. After the abyss, a hero is transformed.

To get to the transformation, you must go through the abyss. To get to transformation, there has to be a death. There has to be a goodbye to the old self. And it's terrifying.

Cracking open our beliefs provokes a heck of a lot of fearfulness. Freaking fear is always going to be there. The son of a bitch never leaves. Fear is hardwired in our brains, similar to homeostasis. That's right, another brain hurdle for us to climb. I'm telling you, evolving is like defying all odds. We can be mentally prepared to disagree with ourselves and mentally prepared to disagree with loved ones, and then boom—we bump into fear. I figure we could learn best practices on how to cope with fear since we're stuck with it.

Fear resides in the amygdala. The amygdala is fun to say. Amygdala, amygdala, amygdala. The body's reaction to fear begins in the amygdala region of our brain. It then spreads to all other areas of the body. Our fight or flight senses are activated when a real or perceived threat triggers a response in the amygdala. We become hyper-alert; our heart rate rises, our blood pressure rises, our pupils dilate and our breathing accelerates.

The kicker here is the real *or perceived* part. Our amygdala can trigger a fight or flight reaction inside our bodies to respond to a fake threat. Our brain is telling us there's a threat, yet in actuality, there is not one. Get this, our amygdala sounds its alarm at the sight of a predator *and* when we feel our beliefs are under attack. If someone were to tell me Jesus is a sham, my body would summon the same reflex as if I were locked in a cage with a tiger. I would be in serious danger in only one of those scenarios, but my defenses would go up hardcore in both circumstances. I'd become hyperalert; my heart rate and blood pressure would rise.

Psychologist Daniel Goleman coined the term "amygdala hijacking".[ix] Amygdala hijacking refers to an immediate and intense emotional reaction that's out of proportion to the situation. In other words, it's when someone loses it or seriously overreacts to something or someone. Goleman's term aims to recognize we have an ancient structure in our brain (the amygdala) designed to respond instantaneously to a threat, real or fake.

Stanford neurobiology professor Andrew Huberman describes the brain like so: "Its primary job is to keep us alive, which is why it's so easy to flip people into fear all the time." Do you see what we're dealing with here? Fear is not messing around. Let's get into how we can squash it.

Call me a nerd, but I think our brains are wildly fascinating. Based on scientific studies of neurology, regularly expressing gratitude up and changes the molecular structure of our brains. Production of dopamine and serotonin increases when we focus on the things that spark joy. Thankfulness acts as a lubricant to our brain; it soothes and calms us. Think moisturizer, but for inside our noggins.

When I allow my mind to linger on what I am afraid of in a given situation, I am handing fear a personal invitation to overcome me. But if I choose to center my attention on the things I'm thankful for, suddenly the fears are not nearly as overwhelming. If you're experiencing fear, writing a list of five things you're grateful for can work wonders. We're unable to think straight when we are afraid; our brain tells us we're in a cage with a tiger, even if we're not. So often our body is in fight-or-flight mode unnecessarily. Gratefulness can remove us from the cages we put ourselves in and bring us back into our bodies.

In most cases we fear the worst possible outcome when the worst possible outcome has not happened yet—and, possibly, never will occur. More so, fear is *expecting* the worst possible outcome of a situation to happen, when it may never actually come to fruition. (If it does, we have to suffer by fretting twice!) Further, there are events we perceive to be scary that can flip into a positive.

My belief system imploding on itself was particularly frightening for me regarding my friendships with Christians. I'd built those relationships upon having certain, fundamental ideals in common. And there I was going back on those ideals. The thought of "coming out" to evangelicals by sharing that I was no longer an evangelical was daunting. How would I even begin to tell someone that the radiant faith I used to have—one that they still thoroughly enjoyed—has changed for me? What if those friends do not accept the new me? It was isolating.

I was most panicked to tell one friend in particular. I feared this dear friend would lose all respect for me. I assumed he would think I was a weirdo. I was afraid I'd lose him as a friend forever. By imagining how he could react to the news, I spent my time in an alternate reality. Because actually, this friend received the message and responded in a way I did not see coming. He said not only does he accept my choices, but he is also proud of the deep dive I took into my faith. He said he is proud to call me his friend. I gained *more* of his respect. My friend and I both agreed our friendship is stronger as a result of that conversation. All that fuss over a 100 percent false projection of the future! I projected a negative future in my own make-believe world. Sometimes the fears we have turn on their head and shapeshift into a blessing.

We lose the present when we're scared of the future. Dwelling on fear can be spending time in an alternate reality. Instead of focusing on the worst possible outcome of a situation, try imagining the best possible outcome. It takes practice, but it's doable. Redirection alters our outlook and can even alter our future. What we project for our future can be manifested by our own imagination. Let's focus on the futures we want to see come to fruition.

Unless you have Urbach-Wiethe disease (a genetic disorder in which a person does not feel fear), you're not going to become fearless. You can, however, become resilient. Make a habit of expressing gratitude and expecting the best possible outcomes and see what happens. If you dare…

This brings me to my next tangent: the fear of failure. Failure is a big mama fear in relation to exploration. When we feel the tug to expand past our comfort zones, like clockwork, that fear of failure creeps in. What if the Unknown is not better than the Known?

Arguably the worst thing fear does is get in the way of us trying something new. Fear of failure keeps us at *fine*. I think I speak for the class when I say, we don't want to be *fine*, we want to be *GREAT*. Author Eloise Ristad wrote, "When we give ourselves permission to fail, we, at the same time, give ourselves permission to excel."

Take it from someone who has failed a lot—it sucks. I'm not going to sugarcoat it. But, ironically, failing over and over again can actually help us get past the fear of failing. It sounds backward, but a way to get past the fear of failing is to fail. What happens is, you fail, it sucks, and then you survive. You move on. The world moves on. And then you fail again.

American basketball coach John Wooden said, "Failure isn't fatal, but failure to change might be." Failure is survivable. Stagnancy is what should be feared. The only way we're going to be better at growing is to be better at failing. Better yet, seek out failure. If you are learning to grow, regardless of whether or not you fail first, you win. All of life can be win-win. Put yourself out there and freaking risk it. What are you waiting for? Go for it. Fail. Fall. Fall flat on your face. It will be great. It will hurt, and then it will be great. Because I promise you, you will get back up again.

Now, when you are squashing fears left and right and living free, there will be people in your life who do not get it. Someone resilient can feel super abrasive to someone stuck. I have a splendid idea as to how you can practice failing immediately. Fail at pleasing people.

Beliefs are personal. Our beliefs are for us, not for other people. We cannot hang on to beliefs that are not serving us in order to make other people happy. Often, we are so afraid to stir the pot for the sake of keeping the peace that we neglect our own peace. This might not be what you want to hear, but you will let people down when you evolve. You will. Some folks will look at you differently. It will happen. What matters is the folks who see the new you. The folks who get the new you. The folks who need the new you. Author Lalah Delia said, "I'm not for everyone, but who I am for, I'm for in a major way."

You cannot and will not please everyone. If you are trying to please ten different people, those ten different people will want you to behave in ten different ways. You will be how each person wants you to be, resulting in you being ten different versions of yourself. If you do this enough you will not know which version is the true you. Sometimes we end up subscribing to someone else's view of us. If someone thinks we are quiet, we don't talk much. If someone thinks we are funny, we make jokes. When our very selves are tied to other people, we could lose ourselves as individuals if we're not careful. We could forget who we are.

Kobe Bryant said, "Hate me or love me. It's one or the other, always has been. Hate my game, my swagger. Hate my fadeaway, my hunger. Hate that I'm a veteran. A champion. Hate that. Hate it with all your heart. And hate that I'm loved for the exact same reasons."

Haters are going to hate. If a person is not for you, you do not need their negative energy in your life. If a person does not appreciate the new you, fuck 'em. Whoever's approval you fear losing, whether it's your parent's, friend's, aunt's, sister's, boss', pastor's, lose it. No one's approval is worth sacrificing your own peace and evolution. Throw in the towel of trying to please so you can be the you that's waiting for you on the other side of the abyss.

When you do something new with your life, you enter the Unknown. It's tempting to go back to the Known because we fear what we don't know. The Unknown is a space in which you don't know the outcome. You don't know if you'll fail. You don't know how people are going to respond to your newness. To get out of the abyss and into the transformation, you will have to have a conversation with fear. You've got to dig deep, figure out what you need to do, and do it. I can't make you jump. This is between you and fear. What'll it be?

We're Not Really Strangers

Beau and I got pretty stir crazy six months into quarantine. We splurged on an Airbnb located in one of the most gorgeous getaways in the world: Joshua Tree, California. (Don't @ me, I am obsessed with the desert.) We invited our besties, Tim and Camila, to come with us. The four of us drank sangria, chatted and played games like Settlers of Catan and We're Not Really Strangers.

If you are not familiar with We're Not Really Strangers, it's a game of pure connection. One does not win or lose a round of We're Not Really Strangers, which is a disappointment to my highly competitive side. On each We're Not Really Strangers card there is a conversation starter in the form of a question. The cards are separated into three levels benignly called Level 1, Level 2 and Level 3, though they might as well be called Surface, Knee-Deep and 47 Meters Down.

It was 47 Meters Down and my turn to draw. The instructions were for me to read the card aloud and listen as each person took turns answering it. The question was this: "What do you think I need to let go of?"

Yikes.

Beau hesitated. Then, in love, he said, "Feeling guilty all the time."

Camila's turn. She said, gently, "Trying to be everything to everyone."

Tim paused. "...Insecurities."

Double yikes.

I listened as the people closest to me named the very things I worked so hard to cover up. As a recovering perfectionist, to have three loved ones detect and call out your secrets was like a nightmare come true. My cheeks flushed and I avoided eye contact. I was super embarrassed. I was embarrassed because I knew all of them were right. Then, miraculously, the moment passed. We moved on to the next question. I survived.

It was at that moment when I realized I wasn't fooling anyone. I thought the front of perfection I had put up was working. It wasn't. Beau, Camila and Tim could see right through me. All of them knew I had stuff to work on. Guess what? All of them love all of me, including my flaws. None of them are deterred by my weaknesses. They recognize my imperfections and still want to be my BFF. Knowing this was a relief. Beau, Camila and Tim had not been looking for perfection in me this whole time. And, if I had to guess, God was not looking for perfection in me either. *I* was looking for perfection in me.

I want to let you in on a little secret: zero humans have it all together. Zero. The definition of a human is basically a hot mess. The hot mess mixed with light, love and laughter are exactly what makes our species intriguing and attractive. The reality is that whatever thing we do not want anyone to know about is the very thing calling the shots. We are controlled by what we are hiding and it's what prevents self-acceptance. Perfectionism tries to cover up the parts we do not want to expose. One way or another, those parts are going to pop up—like pimples.

When you are in the presence of a person held back by insecurity, you can tell. Call me hippie-dippy, but you can feel their energy and you can detect their shackles. I didn't want anyone to know my struggles, not even the people closest to me. I made it seem like I was effortlessly skinny. Hiding my imperfections only fed my insecurities. But when we are vulnerable with our struggles, our struggles lose their power. We become more liberated just by bringing our insecurities out from the darkness and into the light. There is freedom in putting everything out there. It's like a release. An exhale. Ironically what helped me break free of perfectionism was letting my imperfections shine.

That night, I opened up to the public about my eating disorder. That's right, I took it to The 'Gram. I intentionally posted a photo of myself in a bikini sans filter and tricky angles, a photo that I would have never posted in a million years. The caption read, "Cheers to kissing perfectionism goodbye. Posting a photo of my actual body is a tiny step towards letting go of constantly trying to prove myself. I'm choosing to love myself as I am."

What is wild is the second I posted that post, I felt so much more confident. That photo got three times as many likes as the photos I curated to appear mini and sexy. I think this is because people could tell. They could feel the energy shift through the screen. They could detect my unshackling.

I assumed that I was alone in suffering from body dysmorphia. Yet lots and lots of my friends texted me and said they dealt with the same issue. Turns out there are more folks on this planet who are driven by a need to prove. Chances are, whatever you're hiding, many other humans are hiding it too.

Please don't feel like you need to broadcast your deepest darkest secrets. There is no need to post on social media if that's not in your wheelhouse. Feel free to start small and share with a close friend who will be gentle with your heart. Again, there's no pressure. The point of vulnerability is to remove the pressure. We are all humans. We are all in this together.

Another time, I was scheduled to attend a small, socially distanced gathering (because Covid) at Zuma Beach for a friend's birthday. The agenda was for us to lounge, snack and play We're Not Really Strangers. As someone who is not a big fan of sand or of being called out on my shit, I went back and forth on if I should flake. Ultimately my people-pleasing tendencies won out in the end; I sucked it up and endured the one-hour trek from Weho to Malibu to celebrate my dear friend, Andrea.

There were six of us friends sitting in a spaced-out circle on the beach. It was my turn to pull a question card. I read the card aloud to the group. Again, I was instructed to listen as each person went around and took turns answering. This time the question was: What do you think I should know about myself that perhaps I'm unaware of?

Here we go again.

My gut reaction was nerves. I braced myself to receive critical feedback. I'd been here once before. At best, I anticipated each person alternating between saying I needed to wash my hair more or that I talked too much (both true). Instead, as if in cahoots, Andrea and all of the other women responded with affirmations.

"Your presence gives others permission to be themselves."

"Your vulnerability is powerful. People are drawn to your rawness."

"You inspire people organically. You are born to be a leader."

"You are beautiful. Inside and out. Your joy is contagious."

"You are creative. You are going to do big things."

Whoa.

I was stunned. Bewildered. Have you ever been blindsided by encouragement? With a sun-kissed forehead and sand in my shorts, I drove home and reflected on how it was probably an ordinary quarantine day for most of the other women in that circle. For me, it was transformative. I felt the trueness and weight of their words lubricate my soul. For one of the first times in my life, I allowed the encouraging words to define me. I think God winked at me.

In the repercussions of Christian culture, I experienced heaps of pain, wounds and damage that nearly destroyed my perception of self. For years, I allowed a negative view of myself to keep me from unlocking my full potential. It was exhausting to think of myself as bad. It took that birthday party by the ocean to push me over the edge (in a good way) to define myself as beautiful, vulnerable, a leader, an inspiration, powerful, joyful, creative, magnetic, *good*.

Both times I played We're Not Really Strangers, I was transformed. (Not a paid ad—swear!) In the first scenario, my weakness was exposed and it was beautiful. In the second, my strengths were exposed and it was beautiful. It is important to surround yourself with people who will shoot straight with you *and* shower you with encouragement. Sometimes our inner circle of friends knows us better than we know ourselves. If you don't know what you need to unlearn, ask a person you trust.

Encouragement is a rare commodity. Not all of us have encouragement on speed dial. I get that. When I feel alone in my struggles, I scour the Interwebs for YouTubers, podcasters and celebrities who dealt with similar trials. It gives me an extra boost to listen to how they made it out and were better for it in the end. Just knowing someone out there has been through the wringer before and made it out on the other side does wonders. It breeds bravery. Although I don't know those people personally, I am still able to draw inspiration from them. It's important to surround ourselves with people who can put courage inside us. Even if that means random people on the Internet.

Peanut Butter Pretzels

Once our panty was whittled down to canned goods and stale pasta, Beau and I drove to our home away from home, Trader Joe's, to restock. At the grocery store, we filled our buggy, or as Beau calls it, "shopping cart," with the necessities: Dunkers, two bottles of Two-Buck Chuck and ice cream. Beau and I tag-teamed the rest. *You grab the zucchini, I'll grab the eggs!*

At the dairy section, I noticed out of my peripheral vision that Beau was not holding up his end of the bargain. I turn to watch the man I love—nowhere near a zucchini—place a bag of peanut butter-filled pretzel nuggets into our buggy. I'm sorry, what? My husband, who *swears* that he does not like peanut butter, voluntarily picking out a peanut butter-filled product… to consume?

I pretended not to notice. I didn't want to embarrass him. My act lasted all but two minutes. After we checked out, riding the elevator down to our car, I couldn't resist.

Me, in the elevator: Um, did I see you place peanut butter pretzels into our buggy?

Beau, in the elevator: Mayyyyyyybeeeeeeeee.

Me, in the elevator: Were those... for you?

Beau, in the elevator: Yesh. *Bashful face*

I had two choices: make fun of him or celebrate him changing his mind. If I went with option number one, I could have said, "I thOuGhT YoU diDn'T LikE pEanUt BuTteRrr." Woof. I chose option number two: dance party. I smiled and started jumping up and down. Beau joined. We did a mini happy dance in the Trader's Joe's elevator. I chanted-slash-sang, "Yes! You changed your mind! You changed your mind! You are opennn to tryinggg peanut bu-uh-terrr!"

Can we all just decide to celebrate each other when we're wrong? I'm for real, let's plan a freaking party. Next time you change your mind, seriously consider throwing a rager. When we uncover better truths than our meh truths and choose to adopt the better truths, it propels us—and the world—forward. That alone is reason enough to cheer. Finding out that something we thought was true is not creates opportunity for growth. It allows us to be closer to our true selves. Cue the confetti.

It's easy for us to congratulate the growth of little ones. We applaud their first steps, praise them for tying a shoelace. We commemorate kiddos for completing grade school. Our society celebrates growth... until adulthood. The milestones we honor in adulthood recognize stagnancy. We are awarded for staying at the same company for years and years. We put a value on experience in the same profession for decades. I want us to cheer for a person each time they quit their job. I want us to do a happy dance if someone in marketing decides to be a baker. Choosing to grow in adulthood is a feat.

Pastor and author Brit Barron said, "We don't need to dig our heels deeper into the sand every time we feel the ground shift. It's okay to shift with it. It's okay to change your mind. It's okay to be a different person than you were ten minutes ago. The ground is shifting and it's okay to let it move you."[x]

I am in love with that quote. It's okay to shift with the sand. When the waves of change are upon you, permit yourself to float forward. Desperately trying to stand your ground is a waste of energy. Stay loose and relaxed. "It's okay to be a different person than you were ten minutes ago." Thank God I'm not the same person I was when I was 18. Thank God I'm not the same person I was last year, and thank God I'm not the same person I was ten minutes ago. I am not stuck in my beliefs. I am not stuck in my beliefs! My beliefs and I are subject to change. Asterisk, SUBJECT TO CHANGE. I will allow myself to shift with the sand.

Beau and I gaze into each other's eyes often and say, "You're not the same person I married five years ago," as a compliment. If you couldn't tell by how much I bring him up, I love my husband. And trust me, he is not the same person I married five years ago. Five years ago, for starters, Beau did not like peanut butter. Eight years ago, when he and I met, Beau was rocking cowboy boots and Wranglers. He was in Kappa Sig. His interests consisted of Texas Tech football and dove hunting. He was stereotypical Texas in the form of a human.

Now, Beau likes peanut butter. Now, Beau dresses in AF1s, jumpsuits, and All Saints sweaters. And now, Beau is far more interested in the Oscars than the Super Bowl. It's not that football wasn't him. It was. It's that movies are more him. It's not that the country attire wasn't him. It's that the Nikes are more him. It's isn't that disliking peanut butter wasn't him. It's that liking peanut butter is more him.

Beau opened up about his changes to one of his old friends from Texas. He shared that he wasn't big into sports anymore. Instantly, Beau's friend said, "LA has brainwashed you."

Beau pondered. Then, he replied, "Quite the opposite, actually." He said he was born and raised in Texas, an environment where everyone and their dog watched football. (Generally speaking.) Football was less of an option and more of indoctrination for him. Beau was borderline brainwashed to believe football should be a part of his identity. Conversely, Los Angeles is a city that shouts, "Be who you want to be!" LA has sportspeople, movie people, creative people, western people, hip people, straight people, queer people, religious people, agnostic people. You get to decide for you. That's the draw.

Los Angeles allowed Beau to choose who he was. He got to choose for himself what he wanted to eat, wear, watch and believe. He discovered he liked some things he thought he didn't like, and he discovered he didn't like some things he thought he liked. Beau entered a city that allowed him to be himself without dirty looks and criticism. He could be a guy and not like sports. He could be a guy and like to be creative. He could be a guy and like to dance and sing. He was free to be himself.

I am in pursuit of obliterating the stigma around shifting with the sand. The narrative that a person has been brainwashed because they have evolved needs to take a hike. And while we're at it, let's flip it around. The real concern, *tragedy* really, is if a person hasn't changed with time. Letting yourself change is what's strong.

Who is down to add an asterisk to their name? Blank Blank*

*Subject to change

Superpowers

Years ago, an experiment was conducted involving five monkeys. The researcher placed the monkeys in a large cage with a ladder. The ladder led to a bundle of hanging bananas which was tied to the top of the cage. The experiment began. One monkey spotted the food and attempted to climb the ladder. However, as he did, the researcher sprayed him with a stream of cold water. The researcher then turned to the other four monkeys and sprayed them as well.

The monkey who had braved the ladder shied away without a banana. All five monkeys were left chilly and wet. Nevertheless, the banana temptation beckoned. Another monkey tried to climb the ladder a few minutes later, and once again, the researcher sprayed him as well as his cage-mates. A third monkey wanted to test his luck. He ascended the ladder, but when this monkey was stopped, it wasn't because of a stream of cold water—this time, the other monkeys stopped him. They wised up. They guessed that if a third monkey climbed the ladder, the cold water would come not just for him but also for them. The other monkeys pulled the third monkey off the ladder and beat him. (Sad!)

The experiment moves to phase two. In phase two, the researcher removed one monkey from the cage and replaced him with a new monkey. The newcomer—naive—spotted the bananas and made an effort to advance up the ladder. Just like the last climber, the other monkeys tugged him down and beat him. Then, the researcher removed a second monkey from the cage—one of the originals—and replaced him with another new monkey. The newest monkey immediately went in for the bananas. And again, all the other monkeys prevented him from climbing the ladder, *including the monkey who had never been sprayed.*

This pattern continued. At the end of the experiment, none of the original monkeys were left. Yet, none of the new monkeys ever grabbed the bananas. Not one of them had been sprayed by the water. Not one of them knew what would happen if they scaled the ladder. It was solely an unspoken understanding between all five of the monkeys not to do it. And that was enough to keep them from trying.

In the spirit of transparency, some sources say this experiment never actually occurred. Regardless of whether it happened or not, I think we can draw a superb lesson from it. Imagine if the researcher interviewed the newer monkeys and asked why they were avoiding the bananas. I bet they'd say, "I don't know. It's just the way it's always been done." Sound familiar?

How many times do we do something in a certain way just because that's how it's always been done? How many times do we do something in a certain way just because that's what everyone else is doing? Challenging social constructs is like challenging centuries of conformity. Sign me up. Rather than copying how it's been done before, what if we looked within for our own new ideas?

Curiosity is a superpower. Get curious. Ask questions—about everything. No question is off-limits. When I say no question, I mean no question. Ask the rawest, true questions you can think of. Ask *why*. Crack yourself open. Let yourself go there.

I have a lot of questions. Like, how come the cultural norm in America is for women to shave their armpits? Women in Europe don't, generally speaking. I hate shaving my armpits. I get ingrown hairs every time. So why do I keep doing it? Because that's how it's always been done? Because I care what people will think? Later, razors. And why is it not more socially acceptable for men to wear dresses? I mean, men in other countries wear robes and dress-like attire, do they not? Isn't that kind of the same thing? A dress is basically just a super long t-shirt. So what if a guy wants to wear a longer tee? Couldn't the norm have easily been flipped to Men Wear Dresses and Women Wear Pants? Again, who is making the rules here? There is no handbook on how to be human to my knowledge. Can't we make our own rules?

And how come the United States has yet to elect a woman President? Women make up half of America's population. Half. In appointing a representative to speak for and decide on behalf of the American people, it seems reasonable for a woman to call the shots half of the time. And why is it that people are still behind bars for possession of marijuana, now that recreational marijuana is legal in 17 states as of April 2021? And why is it that more persons of color— Black, Latinx, Asian, Native American or multiracial—are not in positions of power?

I'll spare you the rest. I hope I never run out of questions.

Curiosity sprouts humility because curiosity comes from a place of not having the answers. Humility is an extremely attractive trait in a human. Humility breeds openness. Openness is a superpower, too. Openness is as important as curiosity is. Curiosity is pointless if we are not open to our findings. Openness leads into empathy. Openness seeks to understand. Openness enters a situation expecting to learn something new. If we can be curious *and* open, we are superheroes. Get curious. Be open. Use your powers.

CarMax

I remember the exact moment I noticed the white people.

I'd visited Austin, Texas, a few times before spending a weekend there at a friend's bachelorette. I always admired Austin. I fantasized about it growing up as it was the nearest big and hipster city within a thousand-mile radius of Little Rock. Austin hosts killer music festivals, and its food scene is to die for. When I heard the bride-to-be chose Austin as her bachelorette destination, I was stoked.

The weekend of the party took place in 2018. I'd lived in Los Angeles for a solid 20 months, and I was on the cusp of transitioning from feeling discombobulated to feeling at home. I had gotten used to street parking and parking tickets. Smoothies costing $14 didn't faze me, nor did stand-still traffic. I had officially acquainted myself with many humans who were not white, wealthy, straight, Republican Christians. I befriended people of various sexual orientations, religions, races and economic classes. Diversity became my new normal.

In Austin, five bridesmaids and one bachelorette dressed up and ordered an Uber-XL to a bar on 7th Street. We were also accompanied by a life-size cardboard cutout of my friend's fiancé (the Maid of Honor's idea). The six of us gals + cardboard fiancé made for quite the spectacle. Upon arrival, our group eyed an open table and I volunteered to grab the first round of drinks. (And by round, I mean one drink for the bachelorette and one drink for me. Rent in LA is expensive, okay.)

The bar was crowded as all get out. I parted the sea with "excuse mes" to open a tab. I ordered two vodka tonics with lime and let the bartender do his thing. I waited and took in my surroundings. There's nothing like people-watching at a bar, am I right? I scanned the packed room of 200ish from my barstool. And that was the exact moment when I noticed the white people. Aside from one dude, every single person in that bar was white. Myself included.

It could have been a weird night or a fluke. Regardless, I was fully taken aback. I thought, *holy shit I do not remember there being so many white people last time I visited Austin.* I did not remember there being that many white people in the South, period. How did I not notice the segregation before? It felt like there was an elephant in the room and no one could see it except for me. But how could I blame them? I'd grown up in Whiteville and did not recognize it to be Whiteville until I escaped. I did not view the places I frequented as segregated, I just saw them as life. *Until now.* Not one sip of alcohol and I was nauseated.

Once I saw the white people I couldn't unsee them.

Speaking of, because the South was all I'd known, I was blind to the vast amount of trucks in the South, too. If I had to put a number on it, I'd guess three out of every ten people own a truck in both Arkansas and Texas. Beau was in that 30 percent; he proudly drove his Ford F-150 to Los Angeles. You don't see many trucks in LA, and for good reason. Have you tried parallel parking a truck in a compact parking spot in Los Angeles? If so, you know it's nearly impossible. Beau had to make 90-point turns to fit inside the spot in our apartment's garage. And, at the DMV, we were charged an environmental fee for not owning a green vehicle. Unless you are in desperate need of a truck for work, I do not recommend it in Cali. After busting both side mirrors, we decided it was time to trade it in.

Beau and I went to CarMax for him to sell his soul, I mean, truck. We knew we wanted a sedan, but we did not know what model or make. Beau and I test drove Hondas and Nissans and Toyotas and Volkswagens. Purchasing a smaller vehicle may have been the last remaining piece needed for Beau to morph into an Angeleno fully. In the end, we drove out of CarMax in a grey

Volkswagen Jetta. Afterwards, I started noticing grey Volkswagen Jettas *everywhere*. At the grocery store, at the gym, at church. I'd point them out to Beau. It wasn't like the Jettas just started appearing on my account. The Jettas had been there the whole time. I was the one not noticing.

Once you see something you did not see before, you can't unsee it.

The thing is, I didn't know what to do with my observations. I noticed the white people like I noticed the Jettas. I silently acknowledged when they were apparent and that was that. I kept my surveillance to myself, not sharing it with any of my friends— white, Black, Asian, anyone. I was thankful to be in diverse spaces in Los Angeles and that was that. I was thankful and that was that.

In the summer of 2020, upon hearing the news of George Floyd's murder, I was appalled. Again, I was nauseated. *I couldn't believe* the blatant display of hatred and corrupt use of power. I watched the video, shook my head in disgust and shed a tear or two. And then I went about my day.

Three days after the footage went viral, I was scheduled to lead a company-wide meeting at the company I worked for. The meeting had been on the calendar for weeks, and the plan was for me to give a refresher on the company's benefits package.

Ahead of the meeting, George Floyd's murder had not been addressed formally in the company. You'd think as the People and Culture Manager I'd be able to detect that morale was low because of recent events. Wrong-o. Checking in with the team before jumping into my work spiel did not even cross my mind.

One of my best friends, Keshia, is Black. Keshia worked at the company, too, and attended the meeting I led. Keshia, rightfully so, assumed I would open up the floor with at least an acknowledgment of the tragic occurrence. So, when I said nothing about the catastrophe whatsoever, she was devastated. To be honest, the tone I led the group with was cheerful… my delivery did not match the energy of the room. But I did not pick up on that until afterward when I received a text from Keshia.

Keshia: Hey, can we talk?

Have you ever gotten one of *those* texts, the ones in which your heart sinks to your toes? The ones in which your gut reaction is, *what did I do?* That's what this was. Two minutes later Keshia and I were FaceTiming.

Keshia told me she was hurting. She had been really shaken up after what happened to George Floyd. The news was a lot for her to process; she had a different reaction than I did. Seeing the video affected her day and week. It was alarming for her. She was worried that what happened to Floyd could happen to her dad, her brother, her cousins. Her. Keshia started to feel unseen when I, one of her best friends, did not so much as send a Slack message to ask how she was doing. And then, to twist the knife, I did not publicly address the pain of the situation in the meeting.

I apologized profusely to Keshia and hung up. When I got off the phone, I processed the conversation. Honestly, fear in the form of defensiveness crept in. I had thoughts like, *Well, I had to be a leader; I can't just be sad about George Floyd in front of the whole company. Or, come on, it's not like I am a racist! I have tons of Black friends. Keshia, for instance, is one of my besties.* (What do I want, a prize?) *And besides, I notice all of the white people!*

Oof.

My heart rate rose, my blood pressure rose, my pupils dilated and my breathing accelerated. That defensive, fight-or-flight reaction bubbled over and spilled out in my mind. I did not pick up on morale being low because morale was not low for me. The video of George Floyd infuriated me, sure, but I behaved as if the news did not affect me. When I watched the video, I did not think once that what happened to Floyd could happen to my husband or my dad or my brother. Because they are not Black. I didn't have to worry about that. Race was not something I thought about. Race was not an obstacle for me. I had no idea my Black friends were in pain because I was blinded by my privilege.

Though George Floyd's murder was a wake-up call for me, police brutality and injustices towards people of color are alarms that have been sounding for hundreds of years. I was just hitting snooze. Although I'd been noticing the white people and had an inner circle of Black friends, I was not participating in the anti-racism movement. I showed no interest in learning how to abolish racism and lasting segregation. Not once did I ask my Black friends about their experience of what it's like to be Black in America.

I began to have uncomfortable conversations. My Black friends shared with me the hurdles they've faced simply due to their Blackness. I listened to story after story after story.

One of my friends is a runner. He said he tries to dress more "white" when he goes on a run. He does this because so often the world views a Black man running outside as a criminal fleeing a crime scene. He knows his life is at stake when he jogs.

Another friend said she would never allow her middle school son to wear a hoodie over his ears. She told me it didn't matter if it was freezing outside, she would not allow it because some people would suspect her son to be a delinquent if he did.

One friend said she never thought she was beautiful because none of the Disney princesses were Black when she was growing up. The definition of beauty she was influenced by was unattainable for her: whiteness.

One friend was on his way home from Bible study. He got pulled over by the cops. He was asked if there were any drugs in the car. He said, "No, sir." The police officer asked him to get out of the car and to put his hands on his head. The policeman threw my friend against the car and handcuffed him.

I heard these stories and I couldn't unhear them. I was seeing the white people, but I wasn't seeing the Black people, really. All of their stories had existed, but I was closed off to them. I was finally absorbing that racism and injustices have been around the entire time I've been alive and long, long before that.

The more I learned about racism, the more I realized how much I did not know about racism. There is so much to uncover and demolish because it's systemic. Fighting systemic racism is not one-and-done. It's work that has to be kept up every single day. It's unlearning personal biases. It's being intentional about where we are spending our money, who we are hiring and voting into leadership positions. Diversity and inclusion is not a side hustle or a hobby; it's a comprehensive radar.

When I noticed the white people, I noticed there was a problem. I just didn't notice that *I* was a part of the problem. If you are white living in America, you are also a part of the problem. America was built on a racist foundation. If you were born in America, you have racism in your makeup. Racism is a disease and the disease has infected all of our systems. Before we can properly treat the disease, we must admit that there is a problem and we are part of it.

Saying "I am not a racist" is like saying "I'm not a white supremacist" or "I'm not a part of the Ku Klux Klan." You may not be a member of the KKK, but you have been affected by the disease of racism. It's not as extreme, sure, but remnants are there and it's making you and everyone around you sicker and sicker. It's easy to view extreme groups as delusional. If our focus is on extreme groups, we could miss something delusional happening inside us. The danger zone is in the in-between, the you and me. Delusions are not limited to extremists. We must ask ourselves, "What am I not seeing?"

After recognizing that we all have bits of racism ingrained, we have to *care* enough to commit to getting it out of our systems. We have to care about the problem to want to fix it. Caring is a choice. In joining the anti-racism movement, we need to be people who care. It's not an overnight solution; it's an exhausting uphill battle. We cannot be performative. We cannot be looking for a gold star of participation. Our egos have to be checked at the door. We are in this together. We have to climb this mountain together.

A white friend of mine in LA, Michel, grew up in middle-of-nowhere Texas. Michel's mother, also white, still lives in middle-of-nowhere Texas and does not have many Black friends in her community. Actually, she does not have *any* Black friends in her circle. During the Black Lives Matter protests, Michel's mom remembered that her daughter's friend group was more diverse. She felt like she might be missing a piece of the puzzle. Michel's mother asked Michel if she knew of anti-racism documentaries or books she could get her hands on to educate herself.

People like Michel's mom are going to change the world. Michel's mom cares. Choosing humility over defensiveness is admirable. All it takes is an ounce of humility to educate yourself on a topic you are afraid of. It's as simple as asking a knowledgeable friend. Emmanuel Acho, the author of *Uncomfortable Conversations with a Black Man,* said, "Unasked questions turn into prejudices." We humans can be quick to make judgments and assumptions about others. If we do not seek out all sides, our unasked questions can be based on a false perception of reality.

Admitting we are a part of the problem is necessary for the problem to be resolved. And caring about the problem is just as necessary for there to be change. Let's dig up our vulnerabilities and expose them in the light. Because when we do that, they lose their power.

God Herself

As I let myself shift with the sand and evolve, I began to see that love is greater than religion. I strayed from a path of rightness in exchange for a path of inclusivity. No longer did I view churches that were All About Love as shallow and watered down. I viewed them as deep and rich because that is what love is. Love is deep and rich.

A friend invited me to an All About Love church in Hollywood. I was nervous and intimidated. All About Love was new and uncomfortable. I got there early before the doors opened. A group of us stood outside the venue as if waiting for a rock concert. I took in my surroundings. The volunteers were dressed in Yeezys and Fear of Gods. I saw a sea of band tees, dainty gold chain necklaces and baggy pants. There was a sign hanging in the foyer that said, "Come as You Are."

Come as you are? You don't have to be straight? You don't have to be cis-gendered? You don't have to be white? Nope, come as you are. What if you have purple hair? What if you have tattoos? What about a nose piercing? Just come as you are. So, you can be...you? Boy, oh boy, was love uncomfortable. And attractive. And contagious.

The doors open. My friend and I were ushered into seats in the dead center of the dimly lit auditorium. Ariana Grande's *Thank You, Next* played loudly over the speakers. Ariana Grande at church? Where am I? I'd never been to a church so... relevant. And fun. Isn't church supposed to be boring? Sorry, I mean, serious?

The worship starts. The worship team was not just singing, they were running. Running around the stage and jumping up and down. And smiling. A lot. Part of the congregation—if you can call them that—began to form a dance pit upfront. I witnessed tens of adults literally jumping for joy. But not me. No, not me. I wouldn't dare. I kept my bottom in my seat, glued to the idea that praising Jesus was supposed to be dignified. Stiff.

The pastor speaks. The pastor, looking fly as all get out, spoke unfamiliar words. He said God created humans to create. He said to live a life of risk, not fear. He said to lean into the discomfort. He said peace comes from within. He said God created women in His image, thus women are without limits. Women can speak. Women can lead. He said God is All About Love.

I was introduced to a form of organized religion where faith and future could coexist. Faith and progress were not mutually exclusive; faith and progress intersected. As a woman, I was celebrated. I was told I could do anything. That church had women drummers, women deacons and women preachers. I watched humans like me, women, leading the church, and I saw that it was good.

I had an awakening. I am not small. I am full of might. I can do big things. I can have big dreams. I am meant for more. I can create. I can take risks. I can be me, unstifled. I was not born to be a follower. I was born to lead.

In so many ways that church was my salvation. And because it brought me such freedom, I wanted to get involved. I figured the least I could do is join the mission in the hope to help others find the empowerment I had found. If I could play even just a tiny part of the production, I wanted in. And so, in I went.

Yet, the more *in* I went, the smaller I got. The more in I went, the more I lost myself.

While the hip church rejected how Apostle Paul refers to women, they emphasized a different, and equivalently limiting, biblically-based concept: spiritual authority.

Right off the bat, the pastors, my "spiritual authority," noticed my vigor. I was entrusted with what was considered the most esteemed volunteer role: caring for the VIPs. The VIPs were the pastors of the church and the celebrities. In retrospect,

I find it a tad unsettling the pastors demanded the same level of adoration and attention as the famous people. But who's to judge?

One Sunday my team was expecting a handful of celebrities. Not going to name drop, but let's just say, I'd be surprised if you have not heard of them. The building had a secret entrance for VIPs. (Pastors entered through the secret entrance too. Yeahhh.) While my fellow VIP volunteers greeted the celebs, my task was to reserve four rows of seats closest to the stage—two rows for the pastors and two rows for the celebrities. Best seats in the house.

I was instructed by my male leader to guard those rows with my life. Yes, sir. Reserving seats might sound like an easy peasy job, but it was much more stressful than you'd think. Since the worship music is like a concert, as soon as the general admission doors open, the GA crowd swarms to the front seats. It was the definition of a shit show.

I was newer; I had not mentally prepared for the rush to come on that strong. To my fright, a rando slipped past me and sat in one of the pastor's seats I was supposed to block. Shoot. I texted my leader to let him know what happened. He texted back and said I needed to gently kick the person out of the seat. I said,

"Okay, cool, will do." And then I thought, *wait, what?* Why exactly am I kicking the kind stranger out of their seat?

I quieted the voice inside me shouting not to do it. I said no to my inner guide and instead followed the orders handed to me by this male "spiritual authority." I asked the human to move.

I hated it. It made me feel icky. It didn't feel good. It didn't feel human.

After the service, I approached the pastor. I had some questions. I wanted to know his reasoning behind asking our team to save those seats. I wanted to know why we had a VIP team at all. Isn't every human a VIP? The pastor said the celebrities were influential. If the celebrities got behind the message of Jesus, they could reach more people with the gospel. So, the leaders of the church designed a VIP team to cater to the influential people. The church leaders did not want a hindrance to come in between a famous person and the message of Jesus. A celebrity could be turned off by a messy space. A celebrity might get annoyed if they walked into a packed auditorium. And for that reason, our serving team cleaned the bathrooms until they were spotless, catered lunch, offered Essentia water and reserved the finest seats. (I didn't ask why the pastors are considered to be VIPs. Oh well. I guess we'll never know.)

I've thought a lot about this. But what I kept going back to is that if the message of Jesus rings true, it will find someone in a mess. It will find someone, even someone with influence, sitting in the back row. Why would we focus on perfecting an experience when imperfections are the very thing that makes our experiences beautiful? Why would we cover up the grit when grit is the very thing that is transformative?

At the end of the conversation, the pastor could tell I wasn't sold. He looked me in the eyes and said, "Trust your leaders."

Trust your leaders. But what if your leader tells you to do something you don't agree with? What if your leader tells you to do something that makes you feel icky?

I tried trusting the leaders. I tried unyielding devotion to them. I tried carrying out orders no matter what, including the ones that made me flinch. I asked permission for things I did not need anyone's permission for other than my own. I kept my mouth shut when I should have spoken up. I allowed myself to be talked down to and demeaned. I let my vulnerabilities be taken advantage of. I said yes to things that I did not have the bandwidth for. I did things out of obligation that did not sit right. In obeying the pastors, performing, I lost gusto for being me. I shrank. I dissipated. In the process of attempting to liberate others, I put myself back in prison. I quieted the voice inside me that told me I was made for more, and for over two years, played a game of Follow the Leaders.

I had an awakening. Again. I can say no. I can get out. I am not stuck. My life is not small. My life is not a performance. It is my life. And I will take it back. I will choose the biggest, truest version of myself.

The Come as You Are church woke me up to my power and purpose, initially. I learned I was capable of creating my own future and internalized countless, worthwhile, life-altering narratives. Yet the more I got involved, the more I saw that "come as you are" doesn't truly mean come as you are. Turns out, it means come as you are and then do what the pastors say. Turns out, it means come as you are and then conform. Come as you are and then perform.

Really, the trendy church's culture wasn't too dissimilar from the orthodox churches' cultures I had been a part of in the past. Except that you could have purple hair. Its atmosphere reeked of control and power. After all that talk about women empowerment, I'd like to think the way I was treated did not have anything to do with the fact that I am a woman. I'd be lying if I said I didn't think it did. Regardless if it did or not, what I do know is what I am accountable for. I am responsible for letting myself fade into the background.

As a woman, as a recovering Fundamentalist woman, an inferiority complex and a firmly established belief in misogyny lingered. Internalizing how the Bible, mainly Paul, speaks about women chipped away at my self-esteem. I believed I was subordinate to and lesser than men. In thinking God wanted me to submit to male figures, I lived with a constant ceiling. I could only take up so much space before I would need to reel back and make room for the men. I could only influence half of the world (other women) and not all of it.

I cannot advocate enough for erasing the mindset that women should be submissive to men, and doing away with yielding to "spiritual authority." I'm going to stick my neck out here and say that spiritual authority is a hoax. Spiritual guidance can be oh so beneficial and helpful, but no one has authority over your life other than you. You are not dependent on a human or an institution for access to the spiritual realm. We are all given the same access to spirituality. By all means, invite advisors who are for you to weigh in on life's difficult decisions. Please do. But the final say is on you and no one else. You get to decide for you.

I am choosing not to disclose the intimate details of what went down behind the scenes of volunteering. To put it in perspective, I hired a therapist to help me process what happened. My therapist told me what I was describing was spiritual abuse. She said, with conviction, I had been spiritually abused. The term "spiritual abuse" caught me off guard. The term sounded so intense, I definitely did not see it coming. It shocked me, so much so that I immediately denied it. I started making excuses. I made excuses for the church as a whole. I made excuses for my abuser. I came to the defense of my abuser. *I came to the defense of my abuser.* I invalidated my own pain.

Spiritual abuse is not a myth; it's legit. It's extremely harmful and damaging, too. I have experienced it and tons of women I know have experienced it. Dan Brennan, MD, said you may have been abused religiously or spiritually if a religious leader has:

- Used scripture or beliefs to humiliate or embarrass you

- Coerced you into giving money or other resources that you didn't want to give

- Forced you to be intimate or have sex that you didn't want

- Made you feel pressured or obligated to do things against your will[xi]

The National Domestic Violence Hotline (NDVC) provides resources for physical, emotional and spiritual abuse. For spiritual abuse, the NDVC's website recommends developing an emotional safety plan. Below is a snapshot summary of their example plan:

- **Seek out supportive people.** A trusted friend or family member can help create a calm atmosphere to think through difficult situations and discuss potential options.

- **Identify and work towards achievable goals.** Achievable goals can be calling a local resource to see what services are available, or talking to an advocate at The Hotline.

- **Remind yourself of your inherent value.** It's never your fault when someone chooses to be abusive to you. Their actions are no reflection of the value you have as a person.

- **Remember that you deserve to be kind to yourself.** Take time every day to practice self-care in order to establish space for peace and emotional safety in your life. Little moments like these can go a long way in helping you think more clearly and make informed decisions.

If you have been spiritually abused, you are not alone. There is a whole community of women (and men) who have been through similar journeys. If you are currently in a spiritually, emotionally or physically abusive situation, I need you to know you are not trapped. You are not stuck.

Misogyny, like racism, is built into the fabric of America. Too many women have been taught directly and indirectly to cater to men. Whether it's flaunting our beauty or shielding our beauty, saying what we're "supposed to" or holding our tongue, we must put an end to it. In the thick of my religious days, I went so far as to self-proclaim to be anti-feminist. How low did my self-esteem have to be for me to be opposed to my own equality? Women, no more dimming our light and our goodness. It's time to turn our brightness all the way up. And stop apologizing for taking up space. (Preaching to myself.) The best gift you can give yourself and others is to shine as bright as you can.

Let's assume there is a God, and that God created us humans in her image. How do we know God isn't a she? Who's to say for certain that the most striking, powerful presence imaginable isn't a woman?

No Because Maturity

A few years ago, I was approved to take two weeks off from work over the holidays. Unlimited PTO, baby. Coming off of a difficult year, I couldn't wait to wind down. Work had been nonstop and I was running out of gas. I was looking forward to 14 straight days of relaxation. Though, alas, due to the two-week agenda I agreed to, I failed to pencil in time to refuel. Please see below for my itinerary.

- December 16th: Fly from LA to Dallas for a friend's engagement

- December 17th: Fly from Dallas to Mexico for a vacation with Beau's family

- December 24th (AM): Fly from Mexico back to Dallas

- December 24th (PM): Drive five hours from Dallas to Little Rock for Christmas with my family

- December 30th: Drive from Little Rock back to Dallas in time for New Year's Eve

- January 1st: Fly from Dallas back to LA; land at 11:00 pm

- January 2nd: Back to work

Why did I do all of this traveling in a span of two weeks, you ask? I could not bear to say no. My friend's fiancé said it would mean the world to him if I could help him with his proposal. How could I say no? Beau's parents offered us an all-expenses-paid vacation to Mexico. How could I say no? My three younger siblings wanted their big sister to spend Christmas with them. How could I say no? I could not fathom disappointing people I loved. So, I said yes. And yes, and yes and yes.

At the risk of sounding like an ungrateful brat, I was pooped after traveling; I was drained and did not feel refreshed. Of course, I was thankful for the opportunities to spend time with my friends and family, but I found it taxing to squeeze everyone in. I was operating on low battery mode. Come to find out, saying yes in order to make people happy with my presence backfired. I was a shell of a person running on ten percent—opposite of present.

Feeling the need to say yes to everything is troublesome. Instantly saying yes to any invitation or request that passes our desk is another form of not making our own decisions. If we say yes to it all, without pausing to think, our time is controlled by the people who ask us to do things. Not having a say in how we spend our time will leave us feeling bitter and resentful. Bitterness and resentment are not a good mix. It's important not to live our lives begrudgingly, hopping from one social contract to another crossing our fingers it all gets canceled... or is that just me?

You can say no. It's okay to set boundaries. It's okay to hold people at a distance. It's okay to deny access to some people. If we show up out of obligation, it's not going to feel good for anyone involved. We have to say no to take care of ourselves. Taking care of yourself is not selfish; it's *mature*. Carving out ample time to love and care for yourself is not selfish.

Loving one another does not equate to selflessness. Selflessness is not an act of love; it's an act of servitude. Obedience. To truly love another, it is not necessary to be selfless; it is necessary to be truly yourself. Only when we are truly ourselves can we truly love another. Filling ourselves up is one of the most loving things we can do for others. We won't be able to love and care for others if our batteries are about to run out of juice. Let's plug ourselves in as long as it takes to get to 100 percent.

I've heard it said, "If it's not a hell yes, it's a no." And I've heard it said, "Your free time is not your availability." I am obsessed with both of those sentiments. Say no with confidence.

There is no need to explain or apologize for taking care of yourself. I like to practice self-care by doing things I love. I love going on long walks, sipping on matcha, singing loudly in the car, listening to podcasts, taking bubble baths, reading, reading while taking bubble baths. All of those activities make me feel animated and the most like myself. Doing things we love reminds us who we are. That stuff is essential if we want to connect to our trueness.

I dream of a beautiful world in which everyone can bring their true selves to the table—no pretending. No facades. No suppressing your needs and desires. No slowly allowing yourself to slip away. If selflessness means smushing yourself down into a ball, it's not worth it. We don't need to shrink; we need to stand tall and strong so that we can lift others up with us. Being true to yourself permits observers to do the same. One of the most generous ways to live is to embrace your true self. People are better the freer they are. We are connected; you being free influences me to be free.

Synagogue

There is something I want to get off my chest. I've been angry a lot lately.

When I hear a transgender human has been beaten to the point of hospitalization, I get angry. When I hear a Black man has been beaten to death by a cop, I get angry. When I hear an Asian-American woman has been shot in a hate crime, an immigrant child has been separated from their mother, a lesbian has been discriminated against, I get angry.

I have decided when this type of anger arises, I do not wish to diminish it. I want it to pass through me and be the fuel that moves me to be the change I hope to see in the world. I will continue to get angry when I hear humans have been cast aside and treated unjustly. I will not grow numb. I will not be unmoved. I will get angry.

The most tragic, disastrous response is to be unmoved and unbothered. The most inhuman response is to remain silent. Indifference is a choice. You can choose to ignore another's groanings. You can pretend another's pain is made up like it doesn't exist. Writing another's hurt off does not make it any less real. The hurt is real. It's there, waiting to be acknowledged and waiting to be addressed. It's bonafide and crying out to be cared for.

Caring about injustices is new for me. I cared about a person's eternal salvation, sure, but I paid minimal concern to the insufferable, devastating experiences minorities were having on the earth. I was too preoccupied with a problem in my imagination (humanity's damnation following death) to care about a legit problem (humanity's mistreatment during life). Then, in the collapse of hell, all of a sudden earth and all of its inhabitants mattered. I flipped a switch from not truly caring to caring deeply. A fake burden lifted from my shoulders and a real burden replaced it.

I used to think living like Jesus meant I'm in a one-piece if everyone is in a bikini. Or I'm sober if everyone is drinking. Now, I think living like Jesus is caring for total strangers. It's loving your enemies. It's defending the oppressed. It's standing up against long-standing unjust systems. It's never violence. It's rebuking the uber-religious and self-righteous. It's looking inward for peace. It's waltzing into a corrupt institution, and when necessary, destroying property.

Jesus was counter-cultural. He introduced progressive views and ideas. He challenged the beliefs that had once been set in stone. He was a revolutionary. Jesus was scoffed at by the ones who thought they had all the answers. Jesus was rejected by the ones who chose to be closed off to his messages. He had haters.

To me, counter-cultural, means curiosity, humility, openness, empathy, love, caring. To me, it means evolution, and when necessary, shifting with the sand.

It matters what you believe about the world. Truth is, if you are looking for evidence to back up your belief that the world is bettering *or worsening* with time, you will find it. We must believe the world is getting better with time. Our core beliefs influence our behaviors. If we believe the world is on a downhill slope, we are unlikely to champion positive change. Because what would be the point if it's regressing no matter what? And our core beliefs have the potential to self-fulfill. If we all believe the world is improving, it just might improve.

Cultural progression is necessary. Slavery used to be legal, now it's not. Interracial marriage used to be illegal, now it's not. Women were not legally permitted to vote, and now they can. The world has made teeny, tiny incremental strides over the past 400 years, but strides nonetheless. Unfortunately, when the world has made strides, followers of Jesus are some of the last to get on board.

In the 1800s, white Christian slave owners used the Ephesians' verse, "Slaves, obey your earthly masters with respect and fear, and with sincerity of heart, just as you would obey Christ," as ammunition to support their wretched custom of keeping Black humans in bondage. Slave owners interpreted the Bible to *justify* their belief in slavery when slavery was legal in America. (Meanwhile, many enslaved Black people clung to the same Bible as their source of hope.) In 1865, when Congress passed a law to abolish slavery, many white Christians adamantly held onto their slaves for as long as possible as the new law contradicted what Paul wrote in Ephesians. Freaking Paul.

If I could petition to remove passages from the Bible, I'd remove one in 1 John about being "In the world, but not of it," and one in Romans where Paul said, "Do not conform to the patterns of this world." I cannot even begin to describe how much harm I, and many other Christians, have caused due to using those two scriptures as excuses to discriminate and exclude. But, if I cannot remove the verses, I would like to offer up a different interpretation. What if the worldly patterns Paul was referring to were not cultural progression, but the worldly patterns of stagnancy, judgment and arrogance? What if John meant to inhabit the world, but not drown in fear, envy and defensiveness? Conforming to sameness is the pattern. Opening yourself up to newness is counter-cultural. Progression in itself is challenging the status quo of the world.

There was a point in which abolishing slavery, interracial marriage and women voting were too "of the world" for Christians. Now, thankfully, evangelical culture has progressed from that point. Drums, tattoos, *dancing* were considered to be "conforming to the patterns of the world." Now, thankfully, we see evangelicals tearing up the dance floor with Hebrew words tattooed on their wrists. All of that cultural progression was necessary, and for the better.

We look back on followers of Jesus from the days of slavery and extreme segregation and oppression and think, "I can't *believe* they used to believe that." And we look back on followers of Jesus from the days of no drums, no tattoos and no dancing, and think, "I can't believe they used to believe *that*." Can you imagine where our world would be today if all of the anti-dancing, anti-tats, anti-drums, pro-oppression, pro-segregation and pro-slavery people did not unlearn what they were taught to believe? We'd be stuck in a rut. Our world is not where it needs to be, but it is moving forward bit by bit. What if the church had not budged from where it was 400 years ago? What if I told you, in 2021, the church is facing a similar crossroads?

When gay marriage was legalized in America, on June 26, 2015, I was not on board. Because I viewed cultural progression in general as a negative, I viewed this court ruling as a negative. I was looking at this decision through the lens of my core belief that the world was getting worse with time. Clearly, I had a change of mind. In all of the instances I listed above, cultural evolution is a positive. Did the world suddenly take a turn for the worse? Or could it be that a more inclusive approach to the LGBTQ+ community is also a positive?

Six years after the court legalized gay marriage, most Christian churches are still reluctant to allow same-sex marriage and welcome members of the LGBTQ+ community into leadership positions. As we've discussed, this is not the first time Christians have been late to the party. I am confident that in years to come these religious institutions will look back on the way they have discriminated against queer folks and think, "I can't believe we used to believe that." I know I do.

There are systems, habits and beliefs in this world that need to crash and burn to be restructured. The systems, habits and beliefs that need to crash and burn cannot crash and burn until we first identify them as problematic. Awareness comes before change. Being aware of the crises in the world is half the battle, while the other half is fighting to solve them. There's a lot of construction in our future. At the risk of sounding like a broken record, it's going to get messier before it gets tidier.

I've got good news and bad news. The bad news is, there is a ton of division and hostility in our world. It is there and I am not suggesting we ignore it. That's the bad news. The good news is, *we* are the solution. We have the power to create change in the world and it starts by changing our hearts. It's time to reevaluate the direction you're headed and course correct. What do you believe about the world? What side of history are you on? Are you feeling uncomfortable? Examine your reactions. Why is it you feel the way you do? Lean in. Get to the bottom of it. Or don't. Let it sit. Just don't let it sit for too long because frankly, this is an urgent matter. People are getting wounded and murdered left and right.

In the meantime, I am choosing to be like Christ. I will continue to get angry in response to human mistreatment and suffering. I will continue to protest, make some noise and act until there is change. Besides, in the synagogue, Jesus went ballistic flipping over tables for much less.

Glad I got that off my chest.

Wildfires

I left out a significant occurrence that took place during our trip to Joshua Tree, California. Beau, Camila, Tim and I booked an Airbnb for two nights, but we only ended up staying for one. The morning after our first sleep, we cooked a breakfast of pancakes, eggs and sausage. By "we" I mean Beau and Tim. Camila and I enjoyed a peaceful reading hour on the couch as the sun rose. After breakfast, the four of us lounged for a good two hours. More reading, some writing, some chatting. 'Twas lovely.

Joshua Tree in the dead of summer is hot—like 115 degrees hot, and that day was no exception. Our Airbnb did not include a pool, so we improvised. The four of us ventured into town to the local Walmart. We purchased two kiddie pools, eight bags of ice (in hindsight we purchased six too many) and matching bandanas. Finally, we were ready to sunbathe. Back at the house, we chilled. Swimmies on, kiddie pools filled, sangrias in hand and selfies galore.

Around three in the afternoon, the sky started falling. I don't know how else to say it except that the sky legitimately started falling. We noticed specs of *something* in our alcoholic beverages. We noticed specs of the same something collecting on the surface of the pools. And at the same time we noticed the sky was falling, we noticed the sky turning a burnt orange color. The sun wasn't even close to setting. The apocalypse seemed like a realistic explanation considering it was 2020.

We packed up and took our party inside to avoid being covered in the falling pieces of sky. After dinner, the four of us played a round of Settlers of Catan, which takes like five hours. Okay, five hours is an exaggeration, but it can take a solid two. Around eight o'clock we decided to check to see if the specs were still coming down. Camila opened the door to step outside and was met with a whiff of smoke. The specs were *ash*. Ash had piled and covered our cars, the outdoor furniture and the ground. It was snowing ash.

Immediately I typed "fire near me" into the Google search bar. Sure enough, there was a wildfire 30 miles away that was at one percent containment. One percent. Beau, Camila, Tim and I debated whether we should still spend the night or if we should head home; 30 miles away wasn't that close but it wasn't that far either. It only smelled like smoke outside and not inside. The area we were in was not labeled as a mandatory evacuation area. Hesitantly, we decided to play another round of Catan.

Towards the end of the game around eleven o'clock, I smelled smoke inside. We all smelled it. There is no way it could be healthy to sleep all night inhaling smoke into our lungs. Ultimately, we made the call to abort. We scrambled to pack up and clean the Airbnb. The four of us got in our cars and drove two hours back to LA.

On the ride home, Beau and I discussed how weird it was to have woken up that morning not knowing that in the evening we'd be departing. We had no idea of the fate in store for us. If we had known, we might not have gone to Walmart or played the second round of Settlers of Catan. Our entire day likely would have looked different. The day would have been much less enjoyable for me as I would have been dreading the car ride home. But because we didn't know the future, we were present.

We don't know a lot of things, but what we do know is that we are here. You are here. I am here. We are here. We don't know the future. We don't know if we have tomorrow, but we know we have right now. Vietnamese monk Thich Nhat Hanh said, "Do not lose yourself in the past. Do not lose yourself in the future. Do not get caught in your worries or fears. Come back to the present moment, and touch life deeply. This is mindfulness."

A life of minimal suffering comes from embracing the present moment. We suffer when we yearn to be someone we're not or somewhere we're not. Suffering can be unnecessary and caging. What if we could experience a life without suffering? What if we could experience heaven on Earth?

To me, heaven on Earth exists when we live life in the present moment. If we can detach from the stories of our past and the anxieties of our future, show up and just Be, peace can arise. Being connected to ourselves and others produces fulfillment, and being present helps connect us to ourselves and others. We don't have to wait for peace, we can experience peace in the Now. You can be complete now. You no longer need to become, you can just be. Swap achieving for Being and attaching for freeing.

A quote I heard one time from Mr. Rogers has stuck with me. In an interview, Mr. Rogers was asked what the most important thing in the world was. He said, "I'm talking to you, so right now you are the most important person to me. Our conversation is the most important thing to me right now." I love that so much. You can tell when a person is present and when a person is not. We make the people we encounter feel loved and valued when we are present. I've been focusing on asking questions and being present when hanging out with a person or group. I remind myself that the conversations I have with the people I am around are top priorities.

As I see it, all we have is the present moment. Because we can't change the past and we do not know what the future holds. I want to be present wherever I am and whoever I am with forever and ever and ever. Who's with me?

Transcend + Include

My *real* birthday, February 23rd, aligns under the Pisces sign. Pisces have prime positive traits such as creativity, generosity and empathy. Like all signs, Pisces have their fair share of negative traits, too. For example, I can be overly trusting and easily swayed. I frequently spot impressionability in the underbelly of my behaviors. I get in these phases. In college, I had a granola girl phase. I wore wraparound headbands, Chacos, and far too many bracelets. Later I had a sneakerhead phase. I wore shoes with soles far too clunky. You see, I get on these kicks. Some kicks last longer than others.

Netflix's *What the Health* prompted my vegan phase. The documentary presents a convincing argument about the harmful effects of dairy and meat and the benefits of a plant-based diet. I was persuaded. Immediately after watching *What the Health*, I decided to alter my lifestyle. I closed my laptop, called my husband and told him the big news. *I'm going vegan.* Just when I thought I couldn't be more LA.

When making dramatic changes to your diet, it is recommended to ease yourself into the changes. I went all in. All at once. Below is a list of what I ate in a typical day before watching the compelling documentary. This was no little adjustment.

I routinely consumed two eggs and two Johnnie O's sausage links for breakfast.

I would eat either a taco, burrito or bowl with chicken and cheese for lunch.

For dinner, I ate salmon or tilapia with rice and veggies.

For dessert, berries and yogurt.

Veganism meant throwing out everything and starting fresh.

The first four weeks I felt phenomenal. In just one month, veganism helped me lose weight, sleep more soundly at night and digest food better than ever. I felt so good I assumed I'd never go back to eating dairy or meat again. In fact, veganism was working so well that I tried to convert Beau. (Beau was not interested.) I started evangelizing to him and anyone who'd listen about my veganism. Four weeks convinced me that veganism was right and that anyone who was not a vegan was wrong.

Since I lacked Beau's support, I found solidarity in fellow vegans. Conversations with the people who ate like me filled me up. The sense of camaraderie gave me the oomph I needed to stick with it in the times I was dying to partake in a charcuterie board. We vegans could relate to each other so much. We were right, *they* (meat-eaters) were wrong.

Then, in the fifth week, veganism stopped working for me. My body started to reject spinach and zucchini and squash and tomatoes. I could not look at a potato without wanting to hurl. I had the most unbearable craving for meat: chicken, beef, squid, octopus, I did not care. My body wanted some nutrients in the form of a piece of meat. Bad.

So I ate meat. And afterward, I was so mad at myself for breaking my vegan streak. Moving forward I only saw two options: get back on the saddle or forget the whole thing. Beau, who is not blind to my habitual all-or-nothing headspace, said, "Why don't you just eat vegan mostly, but when your body tells you to eat an egg, eat an egg?"

Genius.

I looked at veganism as binary. You're either a vegan or you're not. I thought I had to either be a vegan or not pay any attention to how much meat I incorporated into my diet. A much healthier approach would be to keep the benefits I received from eating plant-based foods *and* circle back to the benefits I got from eating meat and dairy. I could eat mostly vegan food. I did not need to throw everything—such as salmon, tilapia, steak, eggs, gouda, feta, yogurt—out completely. *Transcend and include.*

All bodies are different. One body might react swimmingly to an exclusively vegan diet. Strict veganism works for that body. One body might react splendidly to an exclusively carnivorous diet. Carnivorism works for that body. One body might like to eat mostly vegan with the occasional string cheese. One body might like to eat mostly meat with the occasional salad. One body might be allergic to nuts. One body might be lactose intolerant. Food is not binary. Food is not one size fits all.

Fundamentalist Christianity was the longest phase I was in. That one lasted for roughly 20 years. And I was all in. It lasted for so long because it worked well for me for so long. I found a magnificent community with fellow Christians. The sensation of solidarity gave me the oomph I needed to get through life's toughest times. Fundamentalist Christianity worked so well for me, I tried to convert other people to join my exact expression of faith. I wanted others to be like me, to copy how I did life. Because my religion worked so well for me, I thought it was the right religion—the only right religion. And anyone who was not participating in my right religion was wrong.

Christianity, Fundamentalist and Progressive, worked until it didn't. And when it stopped working for me, I thought I had to throw everything out and start fresh. Moving forward I only saw two options: be religious or not be spiritual at all. Be a Christian or be an Atheist. Be far-right or be far-left. Binaries.

So, I tried throwing everything out. I tried hating the Christians, especially the Fundamentalist ones. I tried hating the Republicans, especially the Conservative ones. I tried hating the white people, especially the rich ones. I tried hating the Bible. I tried hating Jesus. I tried hating God. I tried hating my parents. I tried hating myself. I tried hating being borderline brainwashed. All of the hate felt good for about two and a half seconds.

Ditching every part of my background left me with a gaping hole. Rejecting every ounce of my past Christian, Republican, Conservative, naive self, was just another form of believing my newest self was right. I was labeling my old way of being as *wrong*. Newness turned into a right. Sameness turned into a wrong. Black and white. New binaries. I looked backward with disdain.

There were so many aspects of my old world, my old self, that I needed to take with me.

Transcend and include.

In trying to drop Christianity completely, its effects lingered in my habits. For so long I had moved through life under the pretense that I needed to change people. Instead of trying to change gay people into straight people, or non-Christians into

Christians, I tried to change Trump-supporters into Biden-supporters, and Christians to be inclusive. I slowly learned that trying to change people is another form of hate. Hating feels yucky. Trust me, you can skip it. And, as I have learned the hard way, trying to change people is not loving people. (Nor is trying to change people very effective.)

What I have found to be a more beautiful approach is accepting others as they are and accepting ourselves as we are. What can be a forerunner for positive change is when we connect to our core selves. Because at our cores, we are good. The biggest paradigm shifts happen not by talking at people or pointing fingers, but by listening and caring.

So often our beliefs place us into buckets (labels). The Protestant bucket, the Catholic bucket, the Jewish bucket, the Black Lives Matter bucket, the All Lives Matter bucket. I am over separating ourselves. I think it's time we pour out the contents of our buckets into the ocean and come together as one. Labels can be helpful, and labels can be divisive and binary. Man or woman, vegan or non-vegan, Republican or Democrat, heaven or hell, dead or alive, racist or anti-racist. Labeling people as Pisces, Capricorn, Cancer, is super easy to do. Another negative trait of Pisces is that they are *closed off*. That used to be me, but it is not me anymore. I broke free of that label. You are not a label.

Well, you are one label. As am I. All of us are human.

What if instead of using our beliefs to label ourselves and others, we used our beliefs to *connect* us to ourselves and others? Life is not one size fits all. Everyone is unique. What is working for me does not mean it is working for you. What is not working for me does not mean it is not working for you. Each one of us is on a journey for supernatural peace and hope. We have different ways of expressing that search and that's what's beautiful. We are all in this together. We are one.

Oneness

Everything is connected.

I am connected to you and my people. You are connected to me and your people. Which connects me to your people and you to my people. If I am connected to you and my people, my actions impact you and my people. If you are connected to me and your people, your actions impact me and your people.

When everything is connected, our actions affect everything.

I am connected to my cat. My cat is connected to me. If I neglect to feed her, she suffers. If she (heaven forbid) gets hit by a car, I suffer. I am connected to my plants. My plants are connected to me. If I neglect to water them, they wilt. If they wilt, I am bummed. I am connected to material things. Material things are connected to me. If I smash a piece of my ancestors' fine china onto the floor, the china breaks and is unusable. If the fine china, a family heirloom, is unusable, I am devastated.

I am connected to the earth. The earth is connected to me. If I toss a plastic straw into the landfill, the earth struggles to digest it. If the earth cannot digest the straw, the straw winds up in the ocean. If the ocean overflows with trash, I can no longer enjoy the ocean. How we interact with this planet and its inhabitants causes a ripple effect. The ripples spread out through an infinity symbol, ultimately making their way back to us. A ripple effect and an infinity symbol at the same time.

Our physical bodies are connected to our mental state. Our mental state is connected to our emotional state. If I eat poorly, I lack energy mentally. If I lack energy mentally, I feel unmotivated. Drained. If a friend slaps me in the face to be mean, it stings my cheek and my heart. It stings their hand and their heart too.

Everything is connected.

When one of us is experiencing injustice, it affects all of us. When one of us is without shelter, it affects all of us. When one human is hurting, all of us are hurting. When one animal is in distress, we are in distress. When the earth is groaning, we are groaning. We are all in this together. We are one.

Shema Yisrael is a Jewish prayer in the Torah. It opens with, "Hear O' Israel, the Lord our God, *The Lord is One*." What if God is lurking in the connectivity of it all?

Everything is connected.

Pain, fear, joy, anxiety, celebration, strawberries, kittens, mothers, fathers, molecules, succulents, spiders, stars, rivers, mountains, air, humans. All of this exists in relation to one another. There's an undeniable oneness.

Do you feel it?

Knowing

I've always felt capable of doing big things, but—and this is key—I never did big things. Not really, no, and definitely not intentionally. There have been moments in the past when some big things fell into my lap and I rose to the occasion. I've been asked to take the lead on corporate events, church conferences and volunteer initiatives. I've been asked to mentor, to advise, to steward. I've said yes almost exclusively on all occasions, but—and this is key—they haven't been *my* big things. I played significant roles in someone else's plays. I helped carry out someone else's vision. My life was a footnote in someone else's narrative, and something inside of me longed to write my own script.

Pre-pandemic, I did not pause to listen to my heart over the noise of being a perfect employee, churchgoer, wife, friend, sister, daughter, daughter-in-law, bridesmaid, cat-mom, volunteer, traveler, texter, eater, exerciser. My true state of being was buried deep beneath the hustle of my day-to-day routine. It took a worldwide lockdown to turn up the volume on the inner voices I had shushed.

I must acknowledge my privilege in how I was affected by the pandemic. According to a survey by The Commonwealth Fund, more than half of Latinx and nearly half of Black respondents experienced an economic challenge due to the pandemic—substantially more than the 21 percent of white respondents. The disparate impacts of the pandemic on people of color are undeniable. Unlike so many others, I encountered very few physical hindrances. Beau and I were able to pay for rent, food and toilet paper without missing a beat. My loved ones remained healthy throughout the spread of COVID-19. As a white woman existing alongside a year of record deaths, sicknesses and unemployment, my quarantine struggle was strictly mental and emotional.

For me, the problem was that there was no problem. I was in a job I loved with coworkers I loved at a company I loved. Everything was fine. (I've heard it said that "fine" is another term for "half-dead.") Everything was fine, but a lack of contentment in my career snuck up on me. The opportunity to work my way up the corporate ladder was there if I sought it out, I just didn't want it anymore. The top of the top, Human Resources Executive, no longer excited me. At the end of the day, even in a leadership position, the weight of the company's successes or failures rested on someone else. It wasn't my big thing. It was someone else's big thing. I wanted the risk. I wanted the grit.

A whisper I could barely make out was trying to tell me I was capable of more, but I was too busy being fine. I knew I was powerful and courageous on the inside, but what was reverberating off me on the outside was not matching up. I used to see myself as HR. I slowly started seeing myself as me. I wanted to inspire others to live freely through my writing and by simply being myself. Is that even possible?

Remember how I took a solo vacation to New York? And munched on chips and guac at the Arlo hotel rooftop? It was during that time away that I unlocked my Knowing[xii]. After I checked in at the front desk, I wheeled my luggage into the elevator and pressed the button for the seventh floor. Keycard in hand, I got off on my floor and walked down the hallway towards room 705. The padlock buzzed green, I walked in, shut the wooden door behind me and I cried.

I cried, sobbed really, for an hour straight. The tears streamed and streamed and I did not know when or if they'd stop. It was as if God, my body, mind, heart, soul, were waiting for me to be still. For the first time in years, I paused to listen to my sorrow, grief, pain and chains. I amplified the silence. In the stillness, I made room for joy and acceptance and healing. The hard stuff did not get up and walk out of my heart; tenderness sat next to it. Hope and love sitting with frustration and confusion.

Knees to chest, I curled myself into a ball on the freshly made bed. I closed my eyes and opened my palms. I sank into the deepest parts of me. Past the hubbub of how other people think I should behave and believe and be, I searched for the truth. I searched for my next move. I wrestled with questions like, "Who am I?" and "What am I doing here?" Motionless, I remained until an immeasurable sense of tranquility arose.

I heard,

I Am is here.

I have always been here.

I am for you.

I have always been for you.

You are loved.

You are accepted.

You are good.

You be you and that is all.

You are on the true path.

You are moving forward.

Moving forward is good.

Moving forward is true.

Your job was for a season.

It's time to go.

It's time to write.

It's time to be brave.

Writing is your next move.

Being alone with the intention of being alone shook me. Confronting my thoughts and my fears was uncomfortable, but necessary to get to a space of clarity. Be still and know.[xiii]

In her book, *Untamed*, Glennon Doyle calls that deep clarity her Knowing, and she helped me realize I have a Knowing, too. She describes it like this: "The Knowing feels like warm liquid gold filling my veins and solidifying just enough to make me feel steady... what I learned (even though I am afraid to say it) is that God lives in this deepness inside of me." What if the Knowing Glennon is referring to is the voice of the Divine? Could it be that divinity is within us? What if by simply pausing to listen to our inner compass, we are actually summoning supernatural guidance?

In moments of internal or external chaos, sink into the deepest parts of you. Create space to be alone with the intention of being alone. Do whatever you need to do to be by yourself and tune out the racket. Lock yourself in a closet. Wake up at five in the morning. Go on a walk. Sit on your bed. Turn off your phone. Whatever you do, practice tuning in to the point of discomfort. Get comfortable with the uncomfortable. Open your heart to receive your next move. Make space for clarity to come. Make space for hope to come. Wait for the Knowing to be the loudest voice in your soul.

Ask and you shall receive.[xiv]

A farmer went out to sow his seed. As he was scattering the seed, some fell along the path, and the birds came and ate it up. Some fell on rocky places, where it did not have much soil. It sprang up quickly because the soil was shallow. But when the sun came up, the plants were scorched, and they withered because they had no root. Other seeds fell among thorns, which grew up and choked the plants. Still, other seed fell on good soil, where it produced a crop—a hundred, sixty, or thirty times what was sown. Whoever has ears, let them hear. (Mat 13.4-9 NIV)

Whoever has ears, let them hear. Jesus told the above parable in his Sermon on the Mount. I interpret it to mean if we are listening, a message will come. If we are open to receiving it, clarity will come. To hear what we need—not want, but need—we must become the good soil.

I think our intuition is like the seed. We might hear what we need to hear, but do we put it into action? In the bustle, it's easy for the guidance we feel in our gut to be eaten up by distractions. Do we hear what we need to hear, get distracted and forget? Or, is our intuition scorched by fear? Do we hear what we need to hear, have good intentions, but lack follow-through? Or is the soul-message able to take root within us? When we put the soul-message into action, we are able to produce a crop—a hundred, sixty, or thirty times what was sown.

You are the good soil. Sink into your good soil.

The kicker is making sure the memo does not get lost in translation. Follow-through is what's scariest. The second I stepped off the plane back in LA, I told my friends and fam I was going to quit my job and write a book. I heard, "But how will you make money?" "But you have a great job." "But what if you fail?" "Why not do both?" "But how will you make money?"

Their responses were all... logical. Rational. Undeniable resonance that is soul-deep is not based on logic or reason. It does not need to consult with outside sources. It just knows. The only reply I could think of was, "I don't know how to explain it, but I just know this is my next move." Their fears were not my fears but soon their fears became my fears. I felt supernatural peace for about one week and then anxiety and worry crept in. It took me three months after I received clarity on what I needed to do to actually do it. I had to sink again and again and again to muster up the courage to go with my intuition.

As soon as you step out of your isolation period, tests and challenges are going to come at you from all sides. It's up to you to trust your gut and hold onto the message you heard. Follow through and answer the call. Take risks. Sink and then sink again. The truth will guide you.

I Am is with you.

I Am has always been with you.

I Am is for you.

I Am has always been for you.

It's time to be brave.

Seasons

There is a flow to the planet. All by itself, spring becomes summer and summer becomes fall. Fall becomes winter and winter becomes spring. Seasons are natural. Organic.

Humans are no exception. Our taste buds are for a season. We have our skin for a season, approximately 27 days, and then our skin regenerates into something new. We have our taste buds for a season, and then those fully replace themselves after seven years on average. We have our bones for a season, and then our bones change too, every ten. Evolution is in the composition of the universe.[xv]

There's spring, summer, fall and winter. There's sitting up, crawling, walking, running. One season is not better than the other. Summer is not better than winter, and winter is not better than summer. Crawling is not better than sitting up, and sitting up is not better than walking. In order to get from one season to the next, we must let the season we're in run its course. We cannot first run, but must first learn to sit up, crawl and walk. One season comes before the other. There are transitional periods baked into the universe: fall and spring, crawling and walking.

Let your season run its course. When it's over, thank it, and look forward to the next.

If we stay in a season for too long, we become bitter. We are told to never give up and we are told to stay. Both are noble pursuits. But sometimes, giving up is the strong and brave thing. It's not that we leave a season when it gets hard. We fight through the hard stuff. Life is hard. And after that, if it's time to go, it's time to go. We know when it's time to go.

What if you didn't leave because it got hard? What you left because if you had stayed, you would have lost yourself? What if you didn't leave because you were not strong enough? What if you left because you are strong and can walk now?

We're not meant to crawl forever. Don't ruin a season by staying in it for too long. Leave when the season is still good. Leave on time. When you know it's time to go, don't wait. Go. Trust you.

Reminders

Get curious.

Follow your questions.

Open up your heart.

Attain knowledge.

Fight against ignorance.

Unlearn. Everything.

Put stuff back. Or don't.

Accept (love) others.

Accept (love) yourself.

You, me, we have not arrived.

Enjoy the scenery. Keep

exploring. Humility first. Growth

second. Move with empathy.

Be present.

Be you.

Be still and know.

Sink into your good soil.

Trust your intuition.

Use your powers.

Love, love, love.

Seek.

When you seek, you find.

Because seeking is finding.

True Self

In case you haven't noticed, I like to cuss. It's fun.

I like to drink. Pour me a glass of wine and I am one happy chick.

I like tattoos. I have ten and counting.

I like to hit a weed pen before bed. It helps me sleep.

I like to wear bikinis. Immodest ones.

I like to watch movies. R-rated.

I like avocados.

I like me.

I love me.

It's raining. T-Swift is playing in my headphones, her new stuff. I'm on my bed. I've got my coffee. My cat's curled up at my feet. I feel very much like Sarah the Human. Cute, sweet, clumsy, loud, awkward, fun, fierce, chaotic, loving, compassionate, empathetic, moody, goofy, soft, bold, wild. You know, human.

I wrote the first chapter first and the last chapter last. The writing process turned out to be the abyss I needed to sprout into another identity yet again. Sarah Girouard, Sarah Blake and Sarah the Human are intertwined. Connected. My soul is the glue, the binding agent between all of my names. Each name represents a unique phase in my search for what it means to be me. Without the old versions of myself, I could not have gotten to the new. I'm thankful for all of my seasons. Sarah Girouard was a season, Sarah Blake was a season and Sarah the Human is the Now. If now is the present, tomorrow is the future. When tomorrow comes, now will be the past. Who knows what my next name will be?

I think the true you and the true me exist beneath a mound of beliefs. If we allow ourselves to come out from under the weightiness and just Be, goodness will transpire. Because our true selves are good.

Before we can be our best self, we must be our true self. Because our best self is our true self.

Borderline brainwashed or not, you get to decide for you. As you peel back the layers of who you were influenced to be, you will find who you are. You will find your rawness. When your glasses are wiped, you will see yourself unmuddied. You will see what's good.

Don't forget to be gentle with the old version of you. You couldn't be the new version of you without the old version of you. Thank your past.

You and I are connected by a magical mystery. We are asking the same questions. Questions like, "Who am I?" and "What am I doing here?" are the juice of our existence. I don't know what it/he/she/they *is*. I don't know what to call it/he/she/they. God, the Universe, the Divine, I don't know. Whatever it is, I am connected to it. Whatever it is, I am here for it. Whatever it is, I want to tap into it.

I am connected to you and you are connected to me. The Divine is connected to me, and you are connected to The Divine.

Be still and tap in.

Here's to evolution.

Acknowledgments

To my readers

Thank you for keeping me raw. You gave me the courage to dig deep. Because of you, I was able to be the most authentic me.

To my therapist

Thank you for showing me I'm not broken; I'm human. That I am lacking and I am whole. You encouraged me to keep writing, even though I was in the thick of healing. Thank you.

To my inspirations

Elizabeth Gilbert, Glennon Doyle, Rob Bell, your works cracked me open. You inspired me to make a work of my own.

To my editor

I'll start with the obvious. Without you, this book would be chock-full of typos and grammatical errors. But the validation you imparted on my manuscript—my first ever! —gave me the confidence to rise above self-doubt. In more ways than one, you make me better.

To my first book

You are my dream come true. You are the outcome and all the success I could hope for. You are physical proof that I have it in me to keep fighting. We freaking did it.

To my friends

You know who you are. You believed in me from the get-go. Your texts, DMs, comments, phone chats, got me through. I am overwhelmed with warm fuzzies.

To my husband

I want you to know you are rare. The way you support me to do big things is not normal. Thank you doesn't even begin to cover it. I love you. We are one.

To the Divine

In moments of confusion, you interrupt with clarity. In moments of despair, you cut in with assurance. I do not know much, but I know you are for me. Thank you for moving with me

Notes

Kahneman, Daniel. *Thinking, Fast and Slow.* Farrar, Straus and Giroux, 2011.

ii Morin, Amy. "3 Important Ways Your Childhood Shaped Who You Are." *Psychology Today*, 4 September 2017, https://www.psychologytoday.com/us/blog/what-mentally-strong-people-dont-do/201709/3-important-ways-your-childhood-shaped-who-you-are.

iii Dweck, Carol. Mindset: *The New Psychology of Success.* Ballantine Books, 2007.

iv Lewis, Ralph. "What Actually Is a Belief? And Why Is It So Hard to Change?" *Psychology Today*, 7 October 2018, https://www.psychologytoday.com/us/blog/finding-purpose/201810/what-actually-is-belief-and-why-is-it-so-hard-change.

v Grant, Adam. *Think Again: The Power of Knowing What You Don't Know.* Viking, 2021.

vi 2 Cor 5.17

vii Bell, Rob. *Everything is Spiritual.* St. Martin's Essentials, 2020.

viii Rohr, Richard. *The Divine Dance: The Trinity and Your Transformation.* Whitaker House, 2016.

ix Goleman, Daniel. *Emotional Intelligence: Why It Can Matter More Than IQ.* Random House Publishing Group, 2005.

[x] Barron, Brit. *Worth It: Overcome Your Fears and Embrace the Life You Were Made For.* Broadleaf Books, 2020.

[xi] Brennan, Dan. "Spiritual Abuse: How to Identify it and Find Help." WebMD, 1 December 2020, https://www.webmd.com/mental-health/signs-spiritual-abuse

[xii] Doyle, Glennon. *Untamed.* The Dial Press, 2020.

[xiii] Ps 46.10

[xiv] Mat 7.7

[xv] Bell, Rob. *Everything is Spiritual.* St. Martin's Essentials, 2020.

CPSIA information can be obtained
at www.ICGtesting.com
Printed in the USA
LVHW030836170821
695469LV00009B/1033

9 780578 935287